THE TRUTH ABOUT PERSONAL FINANCE

WHAT THE BIBLE AND THE HISTORIC ACADEMIC RESEARCH SAY IS THE BEST PATH TO GOD HONORING FINANCIAL (IN)DEPENDENCE

BIBLE STUDY

RON D. FISCHER

THE TRUTH ABOUT PERSONAL FINANCE

GUIDING VERSES

Submit to God and be at peace with Him;
In this way prosperity will come to you.
JOB 22:2

You may say to yourself, "My power and the strength of my hands have produced this wealth for me." But remember the LORD your God, for it is He who gives you the ability to produce wealth.
DEUTERONOMY 8:17-18

But their prosperity is not in their own hands.
JOB 21:16

Faith is being sure of what you hope for
and certain of what you do not see.
HEBREWS 11:1

TABLE OF CONTENTS

You can find the accompanying videos to the Bible Study lessons one of two ways:

Go to our website: https://sites.google.com/view/thetruthaboutpersonalfinance

Under the Study Videos tab, select the individual lesson you wish to view.

OR: Go directly to You Tube and search "The Truth About Personal Finance."

Click on the picture of the Book / Bible Study cover.

Sort the videos by Oldest, and the lessons will be in order.

Click on the lesson you wish to view.

You can contact the author at:
truthaboutpersonalfinance@gmail.com

"Disclaimer: Where Bible verses are quoted, and the words or phrases are in ALL CAPS, the emphasis is mine except when referencing the true God's personal name, LORD, or Yahweh."

LESSON 1

THE BLESSINGS AND PROMISES OF GOD

Many, LORD my God, are the wonders You have done, the things You planned for us.
None can compare with You; were I to speak and tell of Your deeds,
they would be too many to declare.

PSALM 40:5

LORD, I have heard of Your fame; I stand in awe of Your deeds,
LORD. Repeat them in our day, in our time make them known.

HABAKKUK 3:2

SEPARATION FROM GOD THROUGH SIN IS THE HUMAN CONDITION

"Surely I was sinful at ________, sinful from the time my mother conceived me." PSALM 51:5

"There is ________ one righteous, not even one." ROMANS 3:10

"For all have sinned and fall ________ of the glory of God." ROMANS 3:23

GOD'S GREATEST PROMISE—SALVATION AND ETERNAL LIFE

"For God so ________ the world that He gave His one and only Son, that ________ believes in Him shall not perish but have eternal life." JOHN 3:16

"Salvation is found in no one else, for there is no other ________ under heaven given to men by which we must be saved." ACTS 4:12

"He who did not ________ His own Son, but gave Him up for us all—how will He not also, along with Him, graciously give us ________ things?" ROMANS 8:32

GOD'S PROMISES NEVER FAIL

"Not one of all the LORD's good promises...failed; ________ one was fulfilled." JOSHUA 21:45

"For no ________ from God will ever fail." LUKE 1:37

"The LORD is trustworthy in all He promises and ________ in all He does." PSALM 145:13

WE CAN PRAY FOR BLESSING AND PROVISION

"'For I know the plans I have for you,' declares the LORD, 'plans to ________ you and not to harm you, plans to give you hope and a future. Then you will call on me (________), and I will listen to you,' declares the LORD." JEREMIAH 29:11-14

"But if you will seek God ________ and plead (pray) with the Almighty, if you are pure and upright, even now He will rouse Himself on your behalf and restore you to your ________ state." JOB 8:5-6

WITH OBEDIENCE COMES BLESSINGS

"Blessed are all who fear the LORD, who walk in ________ to Him. You will eat the fruit of your labor; blessings and ________ will be yours." PSALM 128:1-2

"Keep the Book of the Law always on your lips; meditate on it day and night, so that you may be careful to do ________ written in it. Then you will be ________ and successful." JOSHUA 1:8

GOD PROSPERS US THROUGH GIVING US SUCCESS

"Your beginnings will seem humble, so prosperous will your ________ be." JOB 8:7

"And the LORD your God will ________ you in everything you do." DEUTERONOMY 15:18

"As long as he ________ the LORD, God gave him success." 2 CHRONICLES 26:5

GOD PROSPERS US THROUGH BLESSING US WITH AN ABUNDANT LIFE

"And if all this had been too little, I would have given you even ________." SAMUEL 12:8

CONCLUSION

God desires to bless His faithful people with abundance, prosperity, and success.

"I love those who love Me, and those who seek Me find Me. With Me are riches and honor, wealth and prosperity." **PROVERBS 8:17-18**

"Remember me, O LORD, when you show favor to your people...that I may enjoy the prosperity of your ones." **PSALM 106:4-5**

It must be said that we do not believe in what is referred to as the "prosperity gospel," which says that if you believe in Jesus you will be financially successful. The truth is that the promises of God outlined above are all true, but Christians as well as unbelievers may experience some of the financial trials associated with the consequences of sin.

ACTION STEPS

1. Do you believe that God's greatest promise is fulfilled in Jesus Christ our Savior, and that you receive eternal life through Him?

Reread the first part of this chapter and ask the Holy Spirit to work in your heart to reveal the truth.

2. Do you believe that every promise of God has been or will be fulfilled?

If not, ask God to give you greater faith to trust Him and His Word.

3. Have you been able to see God's blessings and provisions for your life?

Write down some of the blessings and promises God has fulfilled in your life. Take some time to thank Him in prayer for these blessings. Examine your heart, and make sure there is no sin in your life that is blocking His blessing and any prayers of need.

4. Do you believe that God is at the foundation of any successes you've had in life?

Thank Him for these successes, and ask Him to continue to bless your faith walk.

5. God desires to bless us, His faithful people.

If you are struggling to see these blessings in your life, take some time and examine your personal relationship with Jesus Christ. Have you been faithful in hearing, reading, and studying God's Word? Have you been faithful in prayer? Ask Him in prayer to work through the Holy Spirit to make you a more faithful follower, come to Him in prayer concerning your daily needs, and see how God blesses your efforts to trust Him with your needs as you place Him first in your life.

LESSON 2

CHARACTERISTICS OF GOD (JESUS) AND CHARACTERISTICS OF THE WEALTHY—FINANCIALLY (IN)DEPENDENT

"This is how love is made complete among us...
In this world we are like Jesus."
1 JOHN 4:17

"Finally, brothers and sisters, whatever is true, whatever is noble, whatever is right, whatever is pure, whatever is lovely, whatever is admirable—if anything is excellent or praiseworthy—think about such things."
PHILIPPIANS 4:8

CHARACTERISTICS OF GOD (JESUS)

JESUS IS...NEVER CHANGING!

"Jesus Christ is the ______ yesterday and today and forever." HEBREWS 13:8

"I the LORD ______ ______ change." MALACHI 3:6

"But You ______ the same, and Your years will never end." PSALM 102:27

JESUS HAS...INTEGRITY

"We know You ______ a man of integrity." Matthew 22:16 MARK 12:14

"I the LORD have spoken, and I ______ do it." EZEKIEL 17:24

JESUS...SPEAKS THE TRUTH

"He who seeks the glory of The One who sent Him is a Man of truth; there is nothing ______ about Him." 1 JOHN 2:5-6

"For God does not speak—now ______ way, now another." JOB 33:14

"All Your ______ are true." PSALM 119:160

JESUS IS...TRUSTWORTHY AND FAITHFUL

"The LORD is trustworthy in ______ He promises and faithful in all He does." PSALM 145:13

"For the word of the LORD is ______ and true; He is faithful in all He does." PSALM 33:4

JESUS IS...WISE (Omniscient=All Knowing)

"His ______ is profound." JOB 9:4

"For the foolishness of God is ______ than man's wisdom." 1 CORINTHIANS 1:25

"Oh, the ______ of the riches of the wisdom and knowledge of God!" ROMANS 11:33

JESUS IS...FORGIVING

"You are a ______ God." NEHEMIAH 9:17

"The Lord our ______ is merciful and forgiving." DANIEL 9:9

JESUS IS...MERCIFUL AND COMPASSIONATE

"For the LORD your God is gracious and ______." 2 CHRONICLES 30:9

"The LORD is compassionate and ______." PSALM 103:8

JESUS IS...GOOD

"He is ______; His love endures forever." 2 CHRONICLES 7:3

"You are good, and what You ______ is good." PSALM 119:68

"The LORD is good to ______." PSALM 147:1

JESUS IS...GRACIOUS

"Yet the LORD longs to be ______ to you." ISAIAH 30:18

"I always thank God for you because of ______ grace given you in Christ Jesus." 1 CORINTHIANS 1:4

JESUS IS...LOVE

"For His ______ endures forever." 2 CHRONICLES 20:21

"Whoever does not love does not ______ God, because God is love." 1 JOHN 4:8

JESUS IS...PATIENT

"He is patient with you, not wanting anyone to ______, but everyone to come to repentance." 2 PETER 3:9

"I was shown mercy so that in me, the worst of sinners, Christ Jesus might display His ______ patience as an example for those who would believe on Him and receive eternal life. 1 TIMOTHY 1:16

JESUS IS...JUST

"All His ways are ______. A faithful God who does ______ wrong, upright and just is He." DEUTERONOMY 32:4

"Praise and exalt and glorify the King of Heaven, because everything He does is ______ and all His ways are just." DANIEL 4:37

JESUS IS...HOLY

"Among those who approach Me I will ______ Myself holy." LEVITICUS 10:3

"Your ______, O God, are holy." PSALM 77:13

JESUS IS...RIGHTEOUS

"For the ______ is righteous." PSALM 11:7

"The LORD is righteous in ______ His ways." PSALM 145:17

"Christ...offered Himself ______ to God." HEBREWS 9:14

JESUS IS...GENEROUS

"______ good and perfect gift is from above." JAMES 1:17

"...hope in God, who richly ______ us with everything for our enjoyment." 1 TIMOTHY 6:17

"What is man that You are ______ of him, the son of man that You care for him?" PSALM 8:4

JESUS IS...PEACE

"The LORD is ________." JUDGES 6:12

Jesus says, "Peace I leave with you; My ________ I give you." JOHN 14:27

JESUS IS...POWERFUL

"God is ________ in His power." JOB 36:22

"The Sovereign LORD ________ with power." ISAIAH 40:10

JESUS IS...ETERNAL

"He is the ________ God, the eternal King." JEREMIAH 10:10

"His kingdom is an ________ kingdom." DANIEL 4:3

"His dominion is an eternal ________." DANIEL 4:34

THE CHARACTERISTICS OF THE GODLY WEALTHY—FINANCIALLY (IN)DEPENDENT

THE GODLY WEALTHY STRIVE TO BE...DISCIPLINED

"Get wisdom, ________ and understanding." PROVERBS 23:23

"He who ________ discipline comes to poverty." PROVERBS 13:18

"Fools ________ wisdom and discipline." PROVERBS 1:7

THE GODLY WEALTHY STRIVE TO BE...INTENTIONAL

"Consider ________ what you do." 2 CHRONICLES 19:6

"The ________ of the diligent lead surely to abundance, but everyone who is hasty comes only to poverty." PROVERBS 21:5 ESV

THE GODLY WEALTHY STRIVE TO BE...SELF-CONTROLLED

"Teach the older men to be temperate, worthy of respect, ________-________, and sound in faith, in love and in endurance." TITUS 2:2

"It teaches us to say 'No' to ungodliness and __________ passions, and to live self-controlled, upright and godly lives in this present age." TITUS 2:12

THE GODLY WEALTHY STRIVE TO BE...HARD WORKING

"Whatever you do, work at it with __________ your heart, as working for the Lord, not for men." COLOSSIANS 3:23

"Now we ask you, brothers, to respect those who work __________ among you." THESSALONIANS 5:12

THE GODLY WEALTHY STRIVE TO BE...MINDFUL SPENDERS

Jesus says, "Let __________ be wasted." JOHN 6:12

"An upright man gives __________ to his ways." PROVERBS 21:29

THE GODLY WEALTHY STRIVE TO BE...CONSISTENT IN THEIR PROCESS

"Do not conform any longer to the pattern of this world, but be __________ by the renewing of your mind." ROMANS 12:2

"What you have heard from me, keep as a __________ of sound teaching." 2 TIMOTHY 1:13

THE GODLY WEALTHY STRIVE TO HAVE...INTEGRITY

"I know, my God, that you test the heart and are __________ with integrity." 1 CHRONICLES 29:17

"The integrity of the upright __________ them, but the unfaithful are destroyed by their duplicity." PROVERBS 11:3

"Whoever walks in integrity walks __________, but whoever takes crooked paths will be found out." PROVERBS 10:9

THE GODLY WEALTHY STRIVE TO BE...WISE

"The wise in __________ are called discerning." PROVERBS 16:21

"I __________, dwell together with prudence; I possess knowledge and discretion." PROVERBS 8:12

THE GODLY WEALTHY STRIVE TO BE...PERSISTENT AND RESILIENT

"Let us run with perseverance the race __________ out for us." HEBREWS 12:1

"Because you know that the testing of your faith develops . Perseverance must finish its work so that you may be mature and complete, lacking anything." JAMES 1:3-4

THE GODLY WEALTHY STRIVE TO BE...STEADFAST / RESOLUTE

"You will keep in perfect peace him whose mind is , because he trusts in You." Isaiah 26:3

"And the God of all grace...will Himself restore you and you strong, firm and steadfast." 1 PETER 5:10

"Jesus resolutely ..." LUKE 9:51

THE GODLY WEALTHY STRIVE TO BE...RESPONSIBLE

"But the man who has the matter in his own mind, who is under no compulsion but has control over his will...this man also does the right thing." 1 CORINTHIANS 7:37

"A wise man keeps under control." PROVERBS 29:11

"Give an of your management..." LUKE 16:2

THE GODLY WEALTHY STRIVE TO BE...FOCUSED / DETAIL ORIENTED

"Let your eyes look straight ahead, fix your directly before you." PROVERBS 4:25

"Remember this, it in mind, take it to heart." ISAIAH 46:8

"Fix these of mine in your hearts and minds." DEUTERONOMY 11:18

THE GODLY WEALTHY STRIVE TO BE...HONEST / TRUTHFUL

"They are in their dealings." 2 KINGS 22:7

"LORD, do not your eyes for truth?" JEREMIAH 5:3

"Have I not written thirty sayings for you, sayings of counsel and knowledge, teaching you to be and to speak the truth." PROVERBS 22:20-21

THE GODLY WEALTHY STRIVE TO BE...SELF REFLECTING / VALUES ORIENTED

"For where your is, there your heart will be also." MATTHEW 6:21

"As water reflects the face, so a man's __________ reflects the man." PROVERBS 27:19

"Search me, O God, and know my heart...See if there is any __________ way in me, and lead me in the way everlasting." PSALM 139:23-24

THE GODLY WEALTHY STRIVE TO BE...TRUSTWORTHY

"Now it is __________ that those who have been given a __________ must prove faithful." 1 CORINTHIANS 4:2

"Whoever can be trusted with very little can be trusted with __________, and whoever is dishonest with very little will also be dishonest with much." LUKE 16:10

"The LORD... __________ in people who are trustworthy." PROVERBS 12:22

THE GODLY WEALTHY STRIVE TO BE...CONSCIENTIOUS

"So I strive always to __________ my conscience clear before God and man." ACTS 24:6

"Pray for us. We are sure that we have a __________ conscience and desire to live honorably in every way." HEBREWS 13:18

THE GODLY WEALTHY STRIVE TO BE...RESPECTFUL

"Show proper __________ to everyone." 1 PETER 2:17

Jesus says, "So in __________, do to others what you would have them do to you, for this sums up the Law and the Prophets." MATTHEW 7:12

THE GODLY WEALTHY STRIVE TO BE...GENEROUS

"He and His family were devout and God-fearing; he gave __________ to those in need and prayed to God regularly." ACTS 10:2

"Good will __________ to him who is generous." PSALM 112:5

"A generous man will __________; he who refreshes others will himself be refreshed." PROVERBS 11:25

"A generous man will __________ be blessed." PROVERBS 22:9

THE GODLY WEALTHY STRIVE TO BE...SOCIALLY INDIFFERENT

"Teach me way, O LORD, and I will walk in Your truth: give me an undivided heart." PSALM 86:11

"I will give them an heart and put a new Spirit in them...Then they will follow my decrees and be careful to keep my Laws. They will be My people, and I will be their God." EZEKIEL 11:19-20

CONCLUSION

If we are to become more like Jesus and the Financially (In)dependent, we need to emulate their characteristics in our own life.

ACTION STEPS

1. Do you recognize in yourself some of the qualities of Jesus and the wealthy?

Spend some time in self reflection, and ask God to make you a more mature follower of Jesus and more intentional in your financial affairs.

2. Do you understand that it is only through the Holy Spirit that your faith walk will become more like Jesus?

Stay in His Word, be faithful in worship and prayer, and ask Him to make His will, your will as you strive to be the hands and feet of Jesus on earth.

3. Have you incorporated the characteristics of the Financially (In)dependent in your financial affairs? Or are you flying by the seat of your pants?

Pay attention to the upcoming chapters of this book and take the action steps to better emulate the characteristics of the wealthy, and in time become one of them if it aligns with God's will for your life.

LESSON 3

WORK—A BLESSING FROM GOD

"All hard work brings a profit, but mere talk leads only to poverty."
PROVERBS 14:23

GOD IS OUR EXAMPLE WHEN IT COMES TO WORK

Jesus said to them, 'My Father is ______ at His work to this very day, and I too am working."
JOHN 5:17

GOD GIVES MAN WORK FROM THE CREATION OF THE WORLD

"The LORD God took the man and put him in the Garden of Eden to work it and take ______ of it."
GENESIS 2:15

"To Adam He said;...'Cursed is the ground because of you, through painful ______ you will eat food from it all the days of your life. It will produce thorns and thistles for you, and you will eat plants of the field."
GENESIS 3:17-18

GOD PROVIDES US WITH MENTAL, PHYSICAL, AND SPIRITUAL GIFTS

"But each of you has your ______ gift from God, one has this ______, another has that.
1 CORINTHIANS 7:7

"All of these (spiritual gifts) are the work of one and the same Spirit, and He ______ them to each one, just as He determines." 1 CORINTHIANS 12:11

"That was his responsibility because he was ______ at it." 1 CHRONICLES 15:22

"Each of you should ______ whatever gift you have received to ______ others, as faithful stewards of God's grace in its various forms." 1 PETER 4:10

KNOW YOUR STRENGTHS AND SPIRITUAL GIFTS

"Every skilled person to whom the LORD has given ______ and ability to know how to carry out all the ______ ...are to do the work just as the Lord has commanded." EXODUS 36:1

Find Your Fit by Jane Kise, Kevin Johnson, and Karen Eilers

Now, Discover Your Strengths by Marcus Buckingham and Donald Clifton

Network Participant's Guide—Revised by Bruce Bugbee, Don Cousins, with Wendy Seidman

THE CHOICE OF EDUCATION

With each step of increased education lifetime earnings increase!

FIND PURPOSEFUL WORK THAT MATCHES YOUR GIFTS AND EDUCATION

"May the ________ of the LORD our God rest on us; establish the ________ of our hands for us—yes, establish the work of our hands." PSALM 90:17

"A man can do nothing better than to eat and drink and find ________ in his work. This too, I see, is from the hand of God." ECCLESIASTES 2:24

"For we are God's handiwork, created in Christ Jesus to do ________ works, which God prepared in ________ for us to do." EPHESIANS 2:10

BE THANKFUL FOR THE PURPOSEFUL WORK GOD GIVES YOU

"You are to rejoice before the LORD your God in ________ you put your hand to." DEUTERONOMY 12:18

"So I saw that there is ________ better for a person than to enjoy their work, because that is their lot." ECCLESIASTES 3:22

"Moreover, when God gives someone wealth and possessions, and the ability to enjoy them, to accept their ________ and be happy in their ________—this is a gift of God. They seldom reflect on the days of their life, because God keeps them occupied with gladness of heart." ECCLESIASTES 5:19-20

WE WORK TO PROVIDE FOR OUR FAMILY'S NEEDS

"Anyone who does not provide for their relatives, and especially for their own ________, has denied the faith and is worse than an unbeliever." 1 TIMOTHY 5:8

"You will eat the fruit of your ________; blessings and prosperity will be yours." PSALM 128:2

"The LORD your God has ________ you in all the work of your hands." DEUTERONOMY 2:7

GOD DESIRES WORK / LIFE BALANCE

God is our example:

"So on the seventh day He ________ from all His work. Then God blessed the seventh day and made it holy, because on it He rested from ________ the work of creating that He had done" GENESIS 2:2-3

"Six days do your work, but on the seventh day do ________ work, so…you may be refreshed." EXODUS 23:12

"On the first day hold a sacred assembly and do no ________ work." NUMBERS 28:18

GOD DOES NOT APPROVE OF LAZINESS

"We gave you this rule: 'The one who is ________ to work shall not eat.'" 2 THESSALONIANS 3:10

"The cravings of a sluggard will be the death of him, because his hands ________ to work." PROVERBS 21:25

"One who is ________ in his work is brother to the one who destroys." PROVERBS 18:9

"Do not love sleep or you will grow poor, stay ________ and you will have food to spare." PROVERBS 20:13

WORKING HARD BRINGS BLESSINGS

"Go to the ant, you sluggard; consider its ________ and be wise!" PROVERBS 6:6

"Whatever your hand ________ to do, do it with all your might." ECCLESIASTES 9:10

"The workers ________ faithfully." 2 CHRONICLES 34:12

"A sluggard's appetite is never filled, but the desires of the ________ are fully satisfied." PROVERBS 13:4

"Lazy hands make for ________, but diligent hands bring wealth." PROVERBS 10:4

HEZEKIAH: A BIBLICAL EXAMPLE OF HARD WORK

"In everything he undertook…he sought his God and worked ________. And so he prospered." 2 CHRONICLES 31:21

"Do not be deceived: God cannot be mocked. A man ________ what he sows." GALATIANS 6:7

"In everything he did he had ________ success, because the LORD was with him." 1 SAMUEL 18:14

"Tell the righteous it will be ________ with them, for they will enjoy the fruit of their deeds." ISAIAH 3:10

WITHOUT GOD OUR STRIVINGS ARE USELESS

"What do people get for all the toil and ______ strivings with which they labor under the sun? All their days their work is ______ and pain; even at night their minds do not rest. This too is meaningless." ECCLESIASTES 2:22-23

"They will sow wheat but reap thorns; they will ______ themselves out but gain nothing. They will bear the shame of their ______ because of the LORD's fierce anger." JEREMIAH 12:13

OBEY YOUR SUPERVISOR AS IF WORKING FOR THE LORD

"Obey your earthly masters with respect and fear, and with ______ of heart, just as you would obey Christ. Obey them not only to win their favor when their eye is on you, but as slaves of Christ, doing the ______ of God from your heart. Serve wholeheartedly, as if you were ______ the Lord, not people, because you know that the Lord will reward each one for whatever good they do." EPHESIANS 6:5-8

"Obey your earthly masters in ______; and do it, not only when their eye is on you and to curry favor, but with sincerity of heart and ______ for the Lord." COLOSSIANS 3:22

WE DESERVE OUR WAGES

"Now to the one who works, wages are not credited as a gift but as an ______." ROMANS 4:4

"For the worker is ______ his keep." MATTHEW 10:10

BE CONTENT WITH YOUR SALARY

"Then some soldiers ask him, 'And what should we do?' He replied, 'Don't exhort money…be ______ with your pay.'" LUKE 3:14

"'Friend, I am not being unfair to you. Didn't you ______ to work for a denarius? Take your pay and go.'" MATTHEW 20:13-14

HUMAN CAPITAL

Your current and future earnings!

OUR SALARIES WORK MUCH LIKE A BOND WITH BIWEEKLY PAYOUT

Our human ______________ when young allows us to be more stock heavy in our portfolios, while when we are nearing retirement, when our human capital is approaching ______________, your stock holdings need to decrease and bond holdings increase.

CONCLUSIONS

"Moreover, when God gives any man wealth and possessions, and enables him to enjoy them, to accept his lot and be happy in his work—-this is a gift of God. He seldom reflects on the days of his life, because God keeps him occupied with gladness of heart." ECCLESIASTES 5:19

ACTION STEPS

1. Are you currently satisfied in your work, and work as if working for the LORD?

   If not, do you need to find a new job that is more fulfilling?

2. Does your current job match well with your personal strengths, spiritual gifts, and educational background?

   If not, ask the Lord to direct you to more fulfilling work.

3. If you're nearing high school graduation, do you have a plan on how you'll meet the educational needs of your desired area of employment? Are you going to choose a college degree, trade school, or high school diploma?

   The sooner you have a plan the less money you'll waste getting the qualifications you need.

4. Are you using your human capital to its greatest potential?

   If not, ask the Lord to bless you as you fulfill His will in your life.

5. If you don't currently have a job, are you taking steps to find a new job?

   Update your resume, search online job sites, and apply for work until the Lord blesses you with a satisfying and fulfilling position.

LESSON 4

TITHING COMES WITH BLESSINGS

"Teach me Your way, LORD, that I may rely on Your faithfulness:
Give me an undivided heart."
PSALM 86:11

EVERYTHING WE HAVE COMES FROM GOD

"But _______________ comes from God." 1 CORINTHIANS 11:12

"Everything comes from You, and we have given You only what _______________ from Your hand." 1 CHRONICLES 29:14

"LORD our God, all this abundance that we have provided for...Your Holy Name comes from Your hand, and all of it _______________ to You. I know, my God, that You test the heart and are pleased with integrity. All these things I have _______________ willingly and with honest intent. And now I have seen with joy how willingly Your people who are here have given to You. LORD, the God of our fathers...keep these desires and thoughts in the hearts of Your people _______________, and keep their hearts loyal to You." 1 CHRONICLES 29:16-18

GOD WILL COMPLETE HIS MISSION ON EARTH WITH / WITHOUT YOUR MONEY

"And He is not served by human hands, as if He _______________ anything. Rather, He Himself gives everyone life and breath and everything else." ACTS 17:25

WE SHOULD INTENTIONALLY GIVE OUR BEST FIRSTFRUITS

"What should I _______________ to the LORD for all His goodness to me?" PSALM 116:12

"Do not store up for yourselves treasures on earth...But store up for yourselves treasures in _______________... For where your treasure is, there your _______________ will be also." MATTHEW 6:19-21

"You must present as the LORD's portion the _______________ and holiest part of everything given to you. NUMBERS 18:29

"Bring the best of the _______________ of your soil to the house of the LORD your God." EXODUS 34:26

GIVING COMES FROM THE HEART AND GOD LOVES A CHEERFUL GIVER

"Each of you should give what you have decided in your heart to give, not ________ or under compulsion, for God loves a ________ giver." 2 CORINTHIANS 9:7

"All the officials and all the people brought their contributions ________, dropping them into the chest until it was full." 2 CHRONICLES 24:10

"The people rejoiced at the ________ response of their leaders, for they had given ________ and wholeheartedly to the LORD." 2 CHRONICLES 29:9

GIVING COMES FROM THE HEART

"And everyone who was willing and whose heart ________ them came and brought an offering to the LORD." EXODUS 35:21

"You are to receive the offering for Me from everyone whose heart ________ them to give." EXODUS 25:2

"You were the first not only to give but also to have the ________ to do so." 2 CORINTHIANS 8:10

WE SHOULD NOT COME BEFORE THE LORD EMPTY-HANDED

"________ ________ should appear before the LORD empty-handed." EXODUS 23:15 / EXODUS 34:20 / DEUTERONOMY 16:16

"Ascribe to the LORD the glory due His name, bring an ________ and come before Him." 1 CHRONICLES 16:29

OUR GIVING SHOULD BE PROPORTIONAL TO OUR BLESSINGS

"Each of you must bring a gift in ________ to the way the LORD your God has blessed you." DEUTERONOMY 16:17

"For if the willingness is there, the gift is ________ according to what one has, not according to what one does not have." 2 CORINTHIANS 8:12

"On the first day of the week, each one of you should set aside a sum of money in ________ with your income, saving it up." 1 CORINTHIANS 16:2

"We have different gifts, according to the ________ given to each of us. If your gift is...giving, then give generously." ROMANS 12:6 & 8

WE SHOULD TITHE OUR OFFERINGS

Abram "And praise be to the God Most High...Then Abram gave Him a of everything." GENESIS 14:20

Abraham "And Abraham gave Him a of everything." HEBREWS 7:2

Jacob "Then Jacob made a vow...The LORD will be my God...and all that You give me I will give You a ." GENESIS 28:20-22

"The Israelites generously gave the firstfruits of their grain...and all that the fields produced. They brought a great amount, a of everything." 2 CHRONICLES 31:5

"Be sure to set aside a tenth of that your fields produce each year." DEUTERONOMY 14:22

"A tithe of from the land, whether grain from the soil or fruit from the trees, belongs to the LORD...Every tithe of the herd and flock—every tenth animal that passes under the shepherd's rod—will be holy to the LORD." LEVITICUS 27:30 & 32

TITHING COMES WITH BLESSINGS

"Bring the whole tithe into the storehouse, that there may be food in My house. ' Me in this,' says the LORD Almighty, 'and see if I will open the floodgates of heaven and pour out so much that you will not have room enough for it.'" MALACHI 3:10

"Honor the LORD with your wealth, with the firstfruits of all your crops; then your barns will be filled to , and your vats will brim with new wine." PROVERBS 3:9-10

"Since the people began to bring their contributions to the temple of the LORD, we have had enough to eat and plenty to , because the LORD has blessed His people, and this great amount is left over." 2 CHRONICLES 31:10

"The LORD will the heavens, the storehouse of His bounty." DEUTERONOMY 28:12

"Give, and it will be to you. A good measure, pressed down, shaken together and running , will be poured into your lap. For with the measure you use, it will be measured to you." LUKE 6:38

UNREPENTED SIN CAN MAKE OUR OFFERINGS UNACCEPTABLE TO GOD

"'Will a mere mortal rob God? Yet you rob me?' But you ask, 'How are we robbing you?' 'In tithes and .' You are under a curse...because you are robbing me." MALACHI 3:8-9

"Another thing you do: You flood the LORD's altar with tears. You weep and wail because He no longer looks with favor on your offerings or them with pleasure from your hands. You ask, 'Why?' It is because ...you have been unfaithful to her, though she is your partner, the wife of your marriage covenant." MALACHI 2:13-14

"'I am not pleased with you,' says the LORD Almighty, 'and I will accept ______ offering from your hands.'" MALACHI 1:10

"Stop bringing ______ offerings!" ISAIAH 1:13

CONCLUSIONS

Everything we have comes from God. We are only returning to God what is already His in any offering we give. We should be intentional in our giving, bringing our best firstfruits when giving to the Lord. Our gifts to the Lord should be proportional to our blessings, and come from the heart as God loves a cheerful giver. We should try to tithe our offerings, because with tithing, God promises to provide His blessings.

ACTION STEPS

1. Do you realize that all your blessings come from God, and any offering you make to His mission is a return offering?
2. Do you currently tithe (giving 10% back to the LORD)? Did you know God asks you to test Him by tithing, and He promises to bless you as a result?

If you are not currently tithing, make a plan to increase your giving by 1-2% with each raise you receive until you reach the tithe.

3. Do you offer God your firstfruits with intentional giving, or does He get the leftovers?

Make a plan to be intentional in your giving.

4. Is there any unrepented sin in your life that would make your offerings unacceptable to God?

Repent of any known sins, accept His forgiveness, and be at peace with God.

LESSON 5

YOU NEED A BUDGET

"Be sure to know the conditions of your flocks, give careful attention to your herds; For riches do not endure forever."
PROVERBS 27:23-24

YOU NEED A BUDGET IF YOU ARE:

- Living paycheck to paycheck
- Left with no money at the end of the month
- Without any idea of where your monthly income went
- In credit card debt
- Without at least $1000 of emergency savings
- Unable to fund 3-9 months of emergency savings
- Unable to insure your car, home, health, or life
- Unable to tithe God's work
- Unable to invest 15% or more of your salary
- Unable to fund your children's education
- NOT ALREADY FINANCIALLY (IN)DEPENDENT

WHAT IS A BUDGET?

- Reconciles your income and expenses
- Intentional spending that aligns with our values
- Gives you the ability to track every dollar of income and give it a purpose
- Change frivolous spending on Wants to disciplined spending on Needs and Goals.
- Doesn't restrict you, but frees you to match your spending with your values and goals.
- Will lead you to the peace only found through a personal relationship with Jesus Christ and financial (in)dependence with Him.

LIVING PAYCHECK TO PAYCHECK WITH INCREASING CREDIT CARD DEBT IS NO WAY TO LIVE!

"You will eat and not be satisfied; your stomach will still be empty. You will store up but ________ nothing." MICAH 6:14

"They will wear themselves out but ________ nothing." JEREMIAH 12:13

CREATE A BUDGET AND EVALUATE YOUR SPENDING HABITS

"Let us throw off everything that ______ and the sin that so easily entangles." HEBREWS 12:1

"Turn my eyes away from ______ things; preserve my life according to Your word." PSALM 119:37

WE MUST MAKE A CHANGE!

First Admit: "How I hated ______!" PROVERBS 5:12

Second: Keep your eyes from endless consumerism.
"A discerning person keeps wisdom in view, but a fool's eye ______ to the ends of the earth." PROVERBS 17:24

Life before disciplined spending
"At one time we too were foolish, disobedient, deceived and ______ by all kinds of passions and pleasures." TITUS 3:3

WE NEED TO CHANGE FOR OUR BUDGET TO WORK

"Do not ______ to the pattern of this world, but be transformed by the renewing of your mind. Then you will be able to test and approve what God's ______ is, His good pleasing and perfect will." ROMANS 12:2

WE MUST PRACTICE MINDFUL SPENDING UNTIL IT IS A HABIT

The goal is to provide margin in our finances to reach our financial goals.
"No discipline seems ______ at the time, but painful. Later on, however, it produces a harvest of righteousness and ______ for those who have been trained by it." HEBREWS 12:11

MINDFUL SPENDING

"Those who belong to Christ Jesus have ______ the flesh with its passions and desires." GALATIANS 5:24

"It teaches us to say 'No' to ungodliness and worldly passions, and to live ______ - ______, upright and godly lives in this present age." TITUS 2:12

"Be sure you know the condition of your flocks, give careful ______ to your herds (finances); for riches do not endure forever." PROVERBS 27:23-24

"Now this is what the LORD Almighty says: 'Give ______ thought to your ways. You have planted much, but harvested little. You eat, but never have your fill. You put on clothes, but are not warm. You earn wages, only to put them in a purse with ______ in it." HAGGAI 1:5-6

A BUDGET MAKES US INTENTIONAL WITH OUR MONEY

"Be very careful, then, how ________ live—not as unwise but as wise." EPHESIANS 5:15

A DESCRIPTION OF THE FINANCIALLY (IN)DEPENDENT

"He is the kind of person who is ________ thinking about the cost." PROVERBS 28:8

"Whoever loves discipline loves ________." PROVERBS 12:1

"I HAVE THE RIGHT TO SPEND MY MONEY IN ANY WAY I PLEASE!"

If you can meet your financial objectives (goals) and obligations.

"'I have the right to do anything,' you say—but not everything is ________. 'I have the right to do anything'—but I will ________ be mastered by anything." 1 CORINTHIANS 6:12

"Do not think about how to gratify the ________ of the flesh." ROMANS 13:14

"Life does not consist in an ________ of possessions." LUKE 12:15

THE FINANCIALLY (IN)DEPENDENT ARE UNCONCERNED ABOUT APPEARANCES

"One person pretends to be rich, yet has ________; another pretends to be poor, yet has great wealth." PROVERBS 13:7

A BUDGET ALLOWS US TO EVALUATE OUR NEEDS VS WANTS

Most people spend as follows:

"I denied myself nothing my eyes desired; I refused my ________ no pleasure. My heart took delight in all my work, and this was the reward for all my labor." ECCLESIASTES 2:10

"Everyone's toil is for their mouth, yet their appetite is never ________." ECCLESIASTES 6:7

Instead: "Why spend money on what is not bread, and your labor on what does not satisfy? Listen, listen to me, and eat what is good, and you will delight in the ________ of fare." ISAIAH 55:2

"Do not join those who drink too much wine or gorge themselves on meat, for drunkards and ________ become poor, and drowsiness clothes them in rags." PROVERBS 23:20-21

WE NEED A NEW MINDSET WHEN EVALUATING WANTS VS NEEDS

"As for you…you followed the _____ of this world…All of us also lived among them at one time, gratifying the cravings of our _____ and following its desires and thoughts." EPHESIANS 2:1-3

"You were taught, with regard to your former way of life, to put off the old self, which is being corrupted by its deceitful desires; to be made new in the _____ of your minds; and to put on the new self, created to be _____ God in true righteousness and holiness." EPHESIANS 4:22-24

YOUR FAMILY SHOULD AGREE ON YOUR FAMILY BUDGET

"Every…household _____ against itself will not stand." MATTHEW 12:25

"Any…house divided against _____ will fall." LUKE 11:17

JESUS PROMISES TO PROVIDE FOR OUR BUDGETED NEEDS

"Therefore I tell you…So do not _____ saying, 'What shall we eat?' or 'What shall we drink?' or 'What shall we wear?' For the pagans run after all these things, and your Heavenly Father _____ that you need them. But seek first His kingdom and His righteousness, and all these things will be given to you as well." MATTHEW 6:31-33 / LUKE 12:29-31

"The LORD does not _____ the righteous go hungry." PROVERBS 10:17

"And you will _____ nothing." DEUTERONOMY 8:9

BE CONTENT IN YOUR CIRCUMSTANCES

"But godliness with _____ is great gain. For we brought nothing into the world,and we can take nothing out of it. But if we have food and clothing, we will be _____ with that." 1 TIMOTHY 6:6-8

"I know what it is to be in need, and I know what it is to have plenty. I have learned the secret of being content in any and _____ situation, whether living in plenty or want. I can do _____ things through Him who gives me strength." PHILIPPIANS 4:12-13

"God has been gracious to me and I have _____ I need." GENESIS 33:11

"Then Jesus asked them (His disciples), 'When I sent you without purse, bag or sandals, did you _____ anything?' 'Nothing,' they answered." LUKE 22:35

Pray the words of Proverbs 30:8-9
Give me neither poverty nor riches, but give me only my daily bread. Otherwise, I may have too much and disown you and say, 'Who is the LORD?' Or I may become poor and steal, and so dishonor the name of my God."

A BUDGET TRACKS OUR MONEY LEAKS

"Or suppose a woman has ten silver coins and one. Doesn't she light a lamp, sweep the house and search carefully until she finds it?" LUKE 15:8

CONCLUSIONS

If you are living paycheck to paycheck, there is no money left over at the end of the month to meet your goals, you have no idea where your paycheck went, have credit card debt, don't have an emergency fund, are unable to tithe God's work, can't afford appropriate insurance, or are unable to invest 15% of your salary for retirement, YOU NEED A BUDGET!

ACTION STEPS

1. Are you already using a zero based budget (you've given every dollar of your paycheck a job for the month) to meet your financial goals?

If not, make a commitment today to write a budget whether on paper or using an app. Give it a few months of refinement to get your budget working for you.

2. Are you financially (in)dependent, and mindful in your spending? Are you meeting all your financial goals and putting away money for future large expenditures?

If you can truly say yes to these questions, maybe you don't need a zero based budget! Make sure you are covering all the needs described in the first paragraph of this chapter and all your other desired goals before foregoing a budget.

MONTHLY BUDGETING FORM

INCOME:

SELF	PAY PERIOD	#1	#2	#3	
	SPOUSE	#1	#2	#3	

CHARITABLE GIVING (TITHE)
DEBT REDUCTION

SAVINGS	EMERGENCY FUND	
	RETIREMENT FUND	
	COLLEGE FUND	
HOUSING	FIRST MORTGAGE	
	SECOND MORTGAGE	
	RENT	
ESCROW	REAL ESTATE TAXES	
	HOMEOWNERS INSURE	
	REPAIRS/MAINTENANCE	
	FURNITURE/FURNISHINGS	
	OTHER	
UTILITIES	ELECTRICITY	
	WATER	
	GAS/OIL/PROPANE	
	CELL PHONE	
	GARBAGE	
	CABLE/STREAMING	
FOOD	GROCERIES	
	RESTAURANTS	
TRANSPORTATION	CAR PAYMENT	
	CAR PAYMENT	
	GAS/OIL CHANGE	
	TIRES/REPAIRS	
	AUTO INSURANCE	
	LICENSE/TAXES	
	CAR REPLACEMENT	

CLOTHING	ADULTS
	CHILDREN
	LAUNDRY
MEDICAL/HEALTH	HEALTH INSURANCE
	DENTAL INSURANCE
	VISION INSURANCE
	DISABILITY (STD)
	DISABILITY (LTD)
	DOCTOR VISIT COPAY
	DENTAL VISITS
	OPTOMETRIST VISIT
	RX DRUGS
	HEALTH CLUB DUES
PERSONAL	LIFE INSURANCE
	ADULT EDUCATION
	TOILETRIES
	COSMETICS
	HAIR CARE
	CHILD CARE
	BABYSITTER
	SCHOOL TUITION
	SCHOOL SUPPLIES
	CHILD SUPPORT
	ALIMONY
	SUBSCRIPTIONS
	ORGANIZATION DUES
	GIFTS
	MISCELLANEOUS
RECREATIONAL	VEHICLES
	ENTERTAINMENT
	VACATION

LESSON 6

WE ARE STEWARDS OF GOD'S GIFTS

"What is mankind that You are mindful of them, human beings that You care for them: You made them rulers over the works of Your hands; You put everything under their feet."
PSALM 8:4-6

"Guard what has been entrusted to your care."
1 TIMOTHY 6:20

EVERYTHING WAS MADE BY GOD AND BELONGS TO GOD

"Yours, LORD, is the greatness and the power and the glory and the majesty and the splendor, for ________ in heaven and earth is Yours. Yours, LORD, is the kingdom; you are exalted as head over all. ________ and honor come from You; You are the ruler of all things. In Your hands are strength and power to exalt and give strength to all." 1 CHRONICLES 29:11-12

"LORD our God, all this abundance...comes from Your hand, and all of it ________ to you." 1 CHRONICLES 29:16

"But everything ________ from God." 1 CORINTHIANS 11:12

STEWARD=One who manages or looks after another's property.

"What is mankind that You are mindful of them, human beings that You care for them: You made them rulers over the ________ of Your hands; You put everything under their feet." PSALM 8:4-6

"With My great power and outstretched arm I made the earth and its people and the animals that are on it, and I give it to ________ I please." JEREMIAH 27:5

GOD PROMISES TO PROVIDE FOR ALL OUR NEEDS

"The eyes of all look to You, and You give them their food at the proper time. You open Your hand and ________ the desires of every living thing." PSALM 145:15-16

"The LORD replied to them: 'I am sending you grain, new wine and olive oil, ________ to satisfy you fully.'" JOEL 2:19

"The LORD is my shepherd, I ________ nothing." PSALM 23:1

"And God is able to ________ you abundantly, so that in all things at all times, having all that you need, you will abound in every good work." 2 CORINTHIANS 9:8

GOOD STEWARDS EVALUATE WANTS VS NEEDS

"All of us also lived…at one time, gratifying the cravings of our sinful nature and following its and thoughts." EPHESIANS 2:3

Morgan Housel says: "Past a certain level of income, what you need is just what sits below your ego."

GOOD STEWARDS ARE MINDFUL SPENDERS

Provide purses for yourselves that will wear out." LUKE 12:33

WE SHOULD EVALUATE HOW OUR SPENDING AFFECTS THE REST OF OUR FINANCIAL PLAN

Consistently live below your means!

Sarah Stanley Fallah says: "Who can be disciplined about spending regardless of the economy, trends, or where they are in life? Consistency and discipline are the mindful spending behaviors that are most important."

"Desire without is not good—how much more will hasty feet miss the way!" PROVERBS 19:2

Stacy Johnson says: "You can either look rich or be rich, but probably not both."

"One person pretends to be rich, yet has ; another pretends to be poor, yet has great wealth." PROVERBS 13:7

"Those who wear expensive clothes and in luxury are in palaces." LUKE 7:35

"Better to be a nobody and yet have a servant than to be somebody and have no food." PROVERBS 12:9

GOD WILL HOLD OUR SPENDING TO ACCOUNT

"For your ways are in full view of the LORD, and He all your paths." PROVERBS 5:21

Sarah Stanley Fallah says: "The power we have in the marketplace is not spending our resources, including our attention, with any entity that could influence us off the course of achieving our financial goals."

"Jesus told His disciples: 'There was a rich man whose manager was accused of his possessions. So he called him in and asked him, 'What is this I hear about you? Give an account of your management, because you cannot be manager any longer.'" LUKE 16:1-2

"Teach me to do your , for You are my God; may Your good Spirit lead me on level ground." PSALM 143:10

RESPONSIBLE STEWARDS ARE GIVEN INCREASED RESPONSIBILITY

"Whoever has will be ________ more; whoever does not have, even what they have will be taken from them." MARK 4:25 / LUKE 8:18 / LUKE 19:26

"Whoever can be trusted with very little can also be ________ with much...so if you have not been trustworthy in ________ worldly wealth, who will trust you with true riches?" LUKE 16:10-11

"From everyone who has been given much, much will be ________ ; and from the one who has been trusted with much, much more will be asked." LUKE 12:48

Sarah Stanley Fallah says:
"Learn to derive happiness from the journey to wealth, not the appearance of wealth. Experience the constant joy of being in control (with the help of the LORD) of your life and not allowing consumption to control you."

GOD WANTS US TO AVOID THE SINS OF ENVY AND COVETING

"You shall not covet... ________ that belongs to your neighbor." EXODUS 20:17

"I want you to be ________ about what is good, and innocent about what is evil." ROMANS 16:19

Morgan Housel says:
"You might think you want an expensive car, a fancy watch, and a huge house. But I'm telling you, you don't. What you want is respect and admiration from other people, and you think having expensive stuff will bring it. It almost never does—especially from the people you want to respect and admire you."

"And I saw that all toil and all achievement spring from one person's ________ of another. This too is meaningless." ECCLESIASTES 4:4

"Envy ________ the simple." JOB 5:2

"Surely he will have no ________ from his cravings; he cannot save himself by his treasure. Nothing is left for him to devour, his prosperity will not endure." JOB 20:20-21

DON'T BE A SLAVE TO CONSUMERISM AND DEBT

"People are slaves to whatever has ________ them." 2 PETER 2:19

"They ________ ...them although the LORD had ordered them; Do not do as they do.'" 2 KINGS 17:15

"As obedient children, do not conform to the evil desires you had when you lived in ________ . But just as He who called you is holy, so be holy in all you do." 1 PETER 1:14-15

WE MUST HONOR GOD AND OBEY HIS WORD

"As for God, His way is perfect:: The LORD's _____ is flawless; He shields all who take refuge in Him." 2 SAMUEL 22:31 / PSALM 18:30 / PROVERBS 30:5

"You are near, LORD, and all your commands are _____. Long ago I learned from Your statutes that you established them to _____ forever." PSALM 119:151-152

"Who is wise? Let them realize these things. Who is discerning? Let them understand. The ways of the LORD are _____; the righteous _____ in them, but the rebellious stumble in them." HOSEA 14:9

GOD WANTS US TO LIVE DEBT FREE!

God's ways are always right.

"My son (daughter), if you have put up security for your neighbor (taken on a loan for them), if you have been trapped by what you said, ensnared by the words of your mouth. So do this, my son (daughter), to free yourself, since you have fallen into your neighbor's hands: Go—to the point of exhaustion—and give your neighbor no rest! Allow no sleep to your eyes, no slumber to your eyelids. Free yourself, like a gazelle from the hand of the hunter, like a bird from the snare of the fowler." PROVERBS 6:1-5

WHAT DOES GOD SAY REGARDING FREEING YOURSELF FROM DEBT?

"Go to the point of EXHAUSTION, AND...FREE YOURSELF."

"Whoever puts up _____ for a stranger will surely suffer, but whoever refuses to shake hands in a pledge is safe." PROVERBS 11:15

"Let _____ debt remain outstanding." ROMANS 13:8 NIV

"OWE NOTHING TO ANYONE." ROMANS 13:8 NASB

ADVANTAGES OF DISCIPLINED CREDIT CARD USE

WHY DOES GOD SAY WE SHOULD AVOID DEBT?

"Do not be one who shakes hands in a _____ or puts up security for debts; if you lack the means to _____, your very bed will be snatched from under you." PROVERBS 22:26-27

"Will not your _____ suddenly arise? Will they not wake up and make you tremble? Then you will become their prey." HABAKKUK 2:7

"The rich rule over the poor, and the borrower is _____ to the lender." PROVERBS 22:27

"May a creditor seize _____ he has; may strangers plunder the fruits of his labor." PSALM 109:11

AVOID BANKRUPTCY

"When a man...takes an oath to obligate himself by ______, he must ______ break his word but must do everything he said." NUMBERS 30:2

Jesus uses The Parable of the Unmerciful Servant to describe what could be considered a bankruptcy.

"Since he was unable to pay, the Master ordered that...all that he had be ______ to repay the debt." MATTHEW 18:25

DOES DEBT FREE LIVING SEEM UNATTAINABLE TO YOU?

"I will ______ the blind by ways they have not known, along unfamiliar ______ I will guide them." ISAIAH 42:16

"'For My thoughts are not your thoughts, neither are ______ ways My ways,' declares the LORD." ISAIAH 55:8

DEBT REDUCTION MADE SIMPLE BUT NOT EASY—IT TAKES DISCIPLINE

THE SNOWBALL TECHNIQUE

Align your debt paydown in the order of smallest debt balance to greatest debt balance. You go all in on paying down the smallest balance while paying the minimum on all other debt balances.

THE AVALANCHE TECHNIQUE

List the order of debt paydown from the debt with the highest interest rate down to the debt with the lowest interest rate. You go all in on paying down the balance of the highest interest rate account while paying the minimum on all remaining debt accounts.

CONCLUSION: A PERSONAL CHOICE

Listen to God and eliminate your debt or follow the ways of this world of unrelenting consumerism and increasing debt. "No discipline seems pleasant at the time, but painful. Later on, however, it produces a harvest of righteousness and peace for those who have been trained by it." HEBREWS 12:11

ACTION STEPS

1. Do you have consumer debt that you need to deal with?

   Make a debt reduction plan using either the Debt Snowball or Debt Avalanche method. Don't plan to do it tomorrow, do it today! GO TO THE POINT OF EXHAUSTION AND FREE YOURSELF!

2. Are you being a good steward of God's gifts to you, with mindful spending?

   If not, try to become more disciplined in your spending so that it aligns with God's will and your financial plan.

3. Are you living beyond your means trying to keep up with family, friends and neighbors?

   Make a plan to get off the consumerism treadmill.

4. Are you saving for large purchases, so you don't have to go into debt to make them?

   Get out of debt and put that money into an emergency fund and / or large purchase fund for such things as appliances and vehicles.

5. Are you continuing to use credit cards, while trying to reduce your debt?

   Freeze them in some water in the freezer so they are not accessible, or if you can't use credit responsibly and live within your means, cut them up, and close the accounts.

6. Would you be comfortable with God examining your use of money?

   If not, vow to make changes in your use of money today!

The Debt Snowball and Debt Avalanche examples show how finding an extra $100 in your budget to help pay down debt can pay down $14,061.74 of debt in 32-34 months and when debt free, have $636.75/month available to apply to your Emergency Fund or invest for Retirement. Imagine if you found $200 or $300 or more in your budget to apply towards debt reduction how much faster the debt would be eliminated. This single change will get you well on the path to financial (in)dependence. **It should be noted that for simplicity of the calculations these examples did not include the application of the rolling interest into the figures used.

THE DEBT SNOWBALL EXAMPLE**

Item	Interest	Minimum Payment	New Payment	Current Balance
KOHLS	22%	$16.45		$150.99
			$116.45	$34.54
			$34.54	$00.00
DISCOVER	24.5%	$24.39		$275.76
			$106.30	$169.46
			$140.84	$28.62
			$28.62	$00.00
MASTERCARD	16.75%	$53.25		$757.55
			$112.22	$645.33
			$194.09	$451.33
			$194.09	$257.15
			$194.09	$63.06
			$63.06	$00.00
VISA	18.25%	$64.50		$1780.67
			$195.53	$1585.14
			$258.59	$1326.55
			$258.59	$1067.96
			$258.59	$809.37
			$258.59	$550.78
			$258.59	$292.19
			$258.59	$33.60
			$33.60	$ 00.00
AUTO LOAN	3.45%	$378.16		$11,096.77
			$603.15	$10,493.62
			$636.75	$9,856.87
			$636.75	$9,220.12
			$636.75	$8,583.37
			$636.75	$7,946.62
			$636.75	$7,309.87
			$636.75	$6,673.12
			$636.75	$6,036.37
			$636.75	$5,399.62
			$636.75	$4,762.87
			$636.75	$4,126.12
			$636.75	$3,489.37
			$636.75	$2,852.62
			$636.75	$2,215.87
			$636.75	$1,579.12
			$636.75	$942.37
			$636.75	$305.63
			$305.63	$00.00

THE DEBT AVALANCHE REDUCTION METHOD**

Directions: List your debts from the highest interest rate charged to the lowest interest rate charge. As each debt is eliminated add the current payment with the next debt minimum payment to get the next current payment.

Item	Interest	Minimum Payment	New Payment	Current Balance
DISCOVER	24.5%	$24.39		$275.66
			$124.39	$151.27
			$124.39	$26.88
			$26.88	$00.00
KOHLS	22%	$16.45		$150.99
			$113.96	$37.03
			$37.03	$00.00
VISA	18.25%	$64.50		$1780.67
			$168.31	$1612.36
			$205.34	$1407.02
			$205.34	$1201.68
			$205.34	$996.34
			$205.34	$791.00
			$205.34	$585.66
			$205.34	$380.32
			$205.34	$174.98
			$174.98	$00.00
MASTERCARD	16.75%	$53.25		$757.55
			$83.61	$673.94
			$258.59	$415.35
			$258.59	$156.76
			$156.76	$00.00
			$63.06	$00.00
AUTO LOAN	3.45%	$378.16		$11,096.77
			$479.99	$10,616.78
			$636.75	$9,980.03
			$636.75	$9,343.28
			$636.75	$8,706.53
			$636.75	$8,069.78
			$636.75	$7,433.03
			$636.75	$6,796.28
			$636.75	$6,159.53
			$636.75	$5,522.78
			$636.75	$4,886.03
			$636.75	$4,249.28
			$636.75	$3,612.53
			$636.75	$2,975.78
			$636.75	$2,339.03
			$636.75	$1,702.28
			$636.75	$1,065.53
			$636.75	$428.78
			$428.78	$00.00

THE DEBT SNOWBALL REDUCTION METHOD

Directions: List your debts in order of smallest balance to largest balance, without concern for the accounts interest unless two balances are the same, then list the higher interest rate account first. Paying the smallest balance off first gives you quick positive feedback, making it more likely that you will stay with the plan over time. You will devote as much money toward debt payoff as your budget will allow, paying the minimum on all debt except the current debt you are trying to pay off.

Item	Item Interest	Minimum Payment	New Payment	Current Balance

THE DEBT AVALANCHE METHOD

Directions: List your debts from the highest interest rate debt to the lowest interest rate debt. Add the current payment to the next debts minimum payment, and proceed until all debt is eliminated. Continue to pay all debt items minimal payments until eliminated.

Item	Item Interest	Minimum Payment	New Payment	Current Balance

LESSON 7

EMERGENCY FUND: EVERYONE NEEDS FINANCIAL MARGIN

"Blessed is the one who trusts in the LORD, whose confidence is in Him. They will be like a tree planted by water...it does not fear when heat comes...It has no worries in a year of drought and never fails to bear fruit."
JEREMIAH 17:7-8

"Disaster will come upon you, and you will not know how to conjure it away. A calamity will fall upon you that you cannot ward off with a ransom; a catastrophe you cannot foresee will suddenly come upon you."
ISAIAH 47:11

TAKE GOD AT HIS WORD: YOU WILL HAVE TROUBLE

"Yet a man is born to trouble as ______ as sparks fly upward." JOB 5:7

Jesus says, "I have told you these things so that in Me you may have peace. In this world ______ have trouble. But take heart! I have overcome the world." JOHN 16:33

"There will be trouble and distress for ______ HUMAN BEING who does evil." ROMANS 2:9

"So that NO ONE would be unsettled by these trials. For you know quite well that we ARE ______ for them." 1 THESSALONIANS 3:3

TAKE GOD AT HIS WORD: YOU WILL HAVE TROUBLE

"Get ready; be ______, you and all...gathered about you" EZEKIEL 38:7

"Be sure of this: I ______ you today." JEREMIAH 42:19

WHAT IS LIFE LIKE WITHOUT AN EMERGENCY FUND

"In a little more than a year you who feel ______ will tremble; the grape harvest will fail, and the harvest fruit will not come (You'll lose your job). Tremble, you ______ ...you...who feel secure." ISAIAH 32:10-11

"If you do not obey the LORD you God and do not carefully ______ His commands...The LORD will give you an ______ mind, eyes weary with longing, and a despairing heart. You will live in constant suspense, filled with dread both night and day, never ______ of your life. DEUTERONOMY 28:15,65-66

"Be , or your hearts will be weighed down with…the anxieties of life, and THAT DAY WILL CLOSE ON YOU LIKE A TRAP." LUKE 21:34

NEVER AGAIN! NEVER AGAIN WILL I BE WITHOUT AN EMERGENCY FUND

"The LORD is good, a in times of trouble. He cares for those who trust in Him." NAHUM 1:7

"Cast your cares on the LORD and He will you: He will never let the righteous be shaken." PSALM 55:22

"The righteous person may have troubles, but the LORD HIM FROM THEM ALL." PSALM 34 19

"Is anyone among you in trouble? Let them ." JAMES 5:13

GOD THROUGH JOSEPH PROVIDES THE FIRST EMERGENCY FUND

GENESIS 41:15-45:9

A $1000 DOLLAR EMERGENCY FUND

Over 40% of Americans don't have $500 to $1000 dollars saved for an emergency!

- New tires for the car $800-$1000
- Appliance breaks down $500-$1200 each
- Car repair $500+ each repair
- Plumbing pipe disintegrated under concrete slab $5000
- Well needs to be re-drilled $12,000

"But now trouble comes to you, and you are ; it strikes you, and you are dismayed. Should not your piety be your confidence and your ways your hope?" JOB 4:5-6

A FULLY FUNDED EMERGENCY FUND

You are likely to have financial trouble that reaches well beyond that $1000 dollar starter emergency fund. Don't stop saving at a $1000 emergency fund, but fully fund your emergency fund with at least 3-9 months of living expenses.

FULLY FUNDED EMERGENCY SAVINGS = FINANCIAL PEACE

When you live as God directs, having a fully funded emergency fund, and listening and acting on His guidance, you will have financial peace.

"Whoever listens to Me will live in and be at ease, without fear of harm." PROVERBS 1:33

"Have I not kept this in and sealed it in my vaults." DEUTERONOMY 32:24

"Have you entered the storehouses…which I for times of trouble." JOB 38:22-23

CONCLUSION

Take God at His Word: You will have trouble! We all need margin in our lives. Having a fully funded 3-9 month emergency fund in place gives your family peace through financial margin, for the days when things break down and need to be fixed or replaced, or in case you lose your job. Whether your fully funded emergency fund is for 3, 6, or 9 months of budget expenses depends on the stability of your job and finances.

"Get ready; be prepared, you and all…gathered about you." EZEKIEL 38:7
"The LORD is good, a refuge in times of trouble. He cares for those who trust in Him. NAHUM 1:7

ACTION STEPS

1. Do you have at least $1000 set aside in case of an emergency?

If not, examine your budget, eliminate the fluff, and act as quickly as possible to set aside $1000 in a high yield internet banking or money market mutual fund account.

2. Are you in the middle of an all out debt reduction plan?

If so, finish your debt elimination, and use the money that comes available to fully fund your emergency savings for 3-9 months of your current expenses. Or if you prefer, use half the available money to fund your emergency fund and the other half to increase your retirement investments.

LESSON 8

SUCCESSFUL INVESTING PRINCIPLES

"Many, LORD, are asking, 'Who will bring us prosperity?' Let the light of Your face shine on us."
PSALM 4:6

"But remember the LORD your God, for it is He who gives you the ability to produce wealth."
DEUTERONOMY 8:18

"For what they were not told, they will see, and what they have not heard, they will understand"
ISAIAH 52:15

SAVING

The bank savings and online high yield savings accounts are FDIC insured up to $250,000 dollars per account, while money market mutual funds are not insured.

The real returns of money market mutual funds and online high yield savings accounts will at best barely keep up with inflation. So saving can help keep your money from deluding in value, as it would if you placed it under a mattress or buried it in the dirt, but due to inflation will probably never give you a real rate of return.

"You should have put my money on with the bankers, so that when I returned I would have received it back with interest." MATTHEW 25:27

"Saving is a bargain compared to spending. Every dollar earned and spent is subject to taxes. Instead, stash that dollar in a 401k plan and we get to keep the entire dollar, allowing it to grow tax-deferred."
JONATHAN CLEMENTS

INVESTING

Investments are opportunities that have a greater likelihood of being profitable. Investing is taking your savings and buying real company stocks which will pay in the form of dividends or increased value of the corporation, or lending to the government or corporations in the form of bond purchases, that will pay you back your principal plus interest at a rate that will in the long-term exceed inflation.

Investing for the average person should be in the form of owning STOCK, BOND, OR REIT INDEX MUTUAL FUNDS for the long-term. This avenue of investing provides the market return at a minimum of cost, with the immediate advantage of diversification, which of itself will decrease the risk of owning these assets.

Put this money to work ( );' he said, 'until I come back.'" LUKE 19:13

In the Parable of the Talents, two of the men were responsible and invested the money earning a 100% return, as recorded in MATTHEW 25:16-17

"The man who had received the five talents WENT and put his money to work (invested) and gained five more. So also, the one with the two talents (invested and)gained two more."

SPECULATING

Speculation is an investment opportunity where the investment outcome is highly uncertain. Speculating is a form of trying to become wealthy in the short-term, by using methods that are more likely to fail then succeed.

"Don't do such an thing." JUDGES 19:24

Or the words of the angel:

"I have come to you because your path is a reckless one...." NUMBERS 22:32

"Do not wear yourself out to get rich; do not trust your own ." PROVERBS 23:4

"Turn away from godless chatter and the ideas of what is falsely called knowledge." 1 TIMOTHY 6:20

Do not commit more than 10% of your assets to any or all types of speculating behavior.

"Speculation as a rule requires us to be precisely right about the future. We only gain a profit with gold, art or cryptocurrencies if investors are willing to pay more in the future for these non-income producing assets." J DAVID STEIN

GAMBLING

Gambling is an opportunity (I use this term loosely) that has greater likelihood of losing money.

Dr. Kingsley Jones describes a gamble as "a bet of prospective negative return, with reasonable statistical reliability."

"Those who once ate delicacies are in the streets." LAMENTATIONS 4:5

"All are for gain." JEREMIAH 8:10

"Those who work their land will have abundant food, but those who fantasies will have their fill of ." PROVERBS 28:19

"Have nothing to do with godless and old wives' tales; rather, yourself to be godly." 1 TIMOTHY 4:7

INVESTMENT RISK VS REWARD

When it comes to investing there is no free lunch. If you are investing in assets like stocks that have higher payouts, you are receiving those higher payouts as compensation for the additional risk you are taking. On the risk scale from most risky to least risky it goes like this:

Small Cap Growth > Small Cap Value > Mid Cap Growth > Mid Cap Value > Large Cap Growth > Large Cap Value > Long-term Treasury Bonds > Intermediate Term Corporate Bonds > Intermediate Term Treasury Bonds > Short Term Corporate Bonds > Short Term Treasury Bonds

STOCKS

Buying stocks is buying a stake in a company or corporation, with the hope of receiving future value through company growth and dividend payouts. If you were to pick your own stocks for your personal portfolio, you would need to pick a minimum of 10 to 30 stocks among diverse segments of the stock market to be reasonably diversified.

Instead for the average investor, like myself, I would recommend investing in stock index mutual funds for the foundation of your investment portfolio, for their instant diversification. A realistic assumption for stock investments via an index mutual fund or ETF is a maximum drawdown of 60% with a recovery period of up to four years.

WHAT TO DO IN A STOCK MARKET DECLINE

Continue to buy stocks through Dollar-Cost-Averaging all the way to an eventual market rebound.

DO NOT SELL ON THE WAY DOWN OR AT THE BOTTOM OUT OF FEAR!

If the market decline was gut wrenching for you, once the market rebounds, moderate your portfolio by buying bonds to better match your personal risk tolerance.

INTERNATIONAL STOCKS

"If you live in the United States, work in the United States, and get paid in U.S. dollars, you are already making a multilayered bet on the U.S. economy. To be prudent, you should put some of your investment portfolio elsewhere—simply because no one, anywhere can ever know what the future will be at home or abroad." JASON ZWEIG

I tend to agree with the late Jack Bogle when he recommends, "Your exposure to mutual funds investing in foreign markets should not exceed 20% of your equity (stock) portfolio."

STOCK MARKET RECOVERY

An investor needs to realize when they take a loss in the stock market it takes a larger gain to get back to even:

- Lose 10% and it takes 11% gain to get back to even
- Lose 20% and it takes a 25% gain to get back to even
- Lose 50% and it takes a 100% gain to get back to even

Jesus says, "Thus the saying, 'One sows and another reaps' is true. I sent you to reap what you work for. Others have done the hard work, and you have the benefits of their labor." **JOHN 4:37-38**

"Blessed are those who find , those who gain understanding (of how to successfully invest in stocks); for she is more profitable than silver and yields better than gold. She is more precious than rubies; nothing you desire can compare with her." **PROVERBS 3:13-15**

BOND INVESTING

Bonds are a way individual investors can loan money to the U.S. Treasury or individual corporations, with the expectation of receiving your principal in return with agreed upon interest payments, over a specified period.

U.S. Treasury Bonds are considered the safest in the world as they are backed by the full faith of the U.S. government, and as such are considered riskless. Corporate Bonds on the other hand are rated based on the particular corporation's apparent ability to return your principal with interest, without default.

BOND INTEREST RATE RISK

J. David Stein says, "The one thing investors in bonds must understand is: As interest rates go up, the value of bonds (held) goes down, and vice versa as interest rates go down, the value of bonds (held) go up...If a bond is held to maturity this point of price change becomes mute. Maturity is the term used to describe when a bond returns its principal outstanding and stops paying interest."

The higher (i.e. longer) a bond's or bond fund's duration, the more its price will change as interest rates change. More specifically, a 1% increase or decrease in interest rates will cause an individual bond or bond fund/ETF to fall or rise in price by roughly the amount of its duration.

In the case of bonds, their returns are primarily driven by prevailing interest rates at the time the investment is undertaken. The fundamental rule of thumb for investing in bond funds and bond ETFs is that the best estimate of their future return for holding periods of seven years or more is their current SEC yield. In comparing various bond opportunities you need to know: 1) The SEC yield or yield to maturity, 2) The bond duration, 3) The average bond credit quality.

COSTS MATTER

Once again, the late Jack Bogle points out that costs matter, when he says, "In every case and in every bond category, the superior bond funds could have been systematically identified based solely on their lower expense ratios. The lowest-cost bond mutual funds outpaced the highest-cost funds by between +1.0% and 2.2% annually. The average enhancement in return was +1.8% per year."

TREASURY INFLATION PROTECTED SECURITIES (TIPS)

There is one bond sold by the U.S. Treasury known as Treasury Inflation-Protected Securities, or TIPS that are a very useful investment in times of inflation. The government resets the yield of these I-bonds every 6 months. You can purchase this bond online through the U.S. Treasury website for up to $10,000/ year. You must hold this 30 year bond for at least one year, and if sold in the first 5 years, forfeit the last 3 months of interest. I would recommend buying I-bonds direct from the U.S. Treasury rather than buying a TIPS mutual fund, because when using the mutual fund as your primary TIPS investment, there is the real possibility of losing the principal portion of your investment, while buying directly from the Treasury keeps your principal investment safe, with this returned upon sale.

CASH

Cash or cash equivalents is the money kept in your wallet, purse, checking, savings, or money market mutual funds. For the average investor most cash is kept in checking for monthly expenditures or in online high yield savings accounts or money market mutual funds for emergency savings. For the wealthy investor they may keep some cash "on the sidelines" for stock purchases when the market is falling and stocks are at bargain sale prices.

REAL ESTATE OR REITS

Real estate has been shown to be a worthy investment especially when it results in positive cash flow through rental property. The properly purchased rental property should provide enough income in rent to cover the monthly mortgage payments, insurance, maintenance of the property, and provide cash flow to live off or invest in other assets.

REITS are my preferred method of investing in real estate. I, like many, do not have the time or skills to manage my own rental property. But through investing in a REIT Index Mutual Fund I can gain access to the dividends they are required to pay out, from the rental / lease agreements they have under contract. REITs, on the long-term, average a handsome payout of ~10% per year, rivaling the benefits of owning stocks. But with this average payout comes the risk of SEQUENCE OF RETURNS. REITs tend to be a quality investment during inflationary periods. Make sure to hold your REIT Index Fund in a tax advantaged account.

PRECIOUS METALS: SILVER AND GOLD

If you are going to invest in them, and I currently don't, gold and silver are best held as an inflation hedge. "As of June 2019, U.S. stocks had an average 10-year return rate of 12.21 percent, whereas gold had a return rate of only 3.71 percent." Gold will tend to rise in value as inflation kicks in, or in anticipation of a recession.

"How much better to get than gold, to get insight rather than silver!" PROVERBS 16:16

"Choose my instruction instead of silver, rather than choice gold." PROVERBS 8:10

If you choose to invest in gold or silver or other precious metals keep your asset allocation to 5% or less of your portfolio.

CRYPTOCURRENCY

Buying cryptocurrency with the hope of making a profit is nothing but pure speculation. The blockchain technology that it is based on does not create any value in and of itself. Its value is not based on earnings and dividends like stocks, or interest payments from the government or corporations like bonds.

J. David Stein points out that, "With a speculative asset (such as cryptocurrency) there is no way to know if it will rebound or continue to plummet. There isn't a correct price because there is no income to determine if the price is too high or too low." Its value or profit is only found by selling it to someone else who is willing to pay more for it than you did, "the greater fool theory" of investing.

"Let him not deceive himself by what is worthless, for he will get nothing in return." JOB 15:31

"The sleep of a laborer is sweet, whether they eat little or much, but as for the ( ) rich, their abundance permits them sleep." ECCLESIASTES 5:12

YOUR INVESTMENT FOCUS

There is a laundry list of things OUTSIDE OF YOUR CONTROL as an investor to include: "Inflation, the actions of the President, Congress, the Federal Reserve, the economy, tax policy, the actions of either political party, the level of interest rates, etc."

There is also a list of things YOU CAN CONTROL as an investor and these are the areas YOU NEED TO FOCUS ON to include: In the words of Ben Carlson, "How much you save, instituting a comprehensive investment plan, setting a reasonable asset allocation mix, defining you tolerance for risk, keeping your costs and (trading) activity in check, taking advantage of tax-deferred retirement accounts, and making level headed decisions."

THE MIRACLE OF COMPOUND INTEREST

It is TIME IN THE MARKET, not TIMING THE MARKET that produces investing results through the miracle of compound interest.

"Your beginnings will seem humble, so ____________ will your future be." JOB 8:7

"Faith is being ________ of what we hope for and ____________ of what we do not see." HEBREWS 11:1

The secret of getting rich slowly is the miracle of compounding interest!

THE RULE OF 72

The Rule of 72 is a convenient way to predict how many years before your investments will double. What you need to know in order to use this rule is the percentage of your portfolio return.

THE RULE OF 72 RESULTS

Percent Earned	Years to Double Your Investment
1%	72 years
2%	36 years
3%	24 years
4%	18 years
5%	14.4 years
6%	12 years
7%	10.3 years
8%	9 years
9%	8 years
10%	7.2 years
11%	6.55 years
12%	6 years

"So fix our eyes not on what is seen, but on what is ____________." 2 CORINTHIANS 4:18

"What strength do I have that I should still have ________? What prospects, that I should be ____________?" JOB 6:11

THE UNSEEN PROSPECTS OF COMPOUND INTEREST MULTIPLYING YOUR PORTFOLIO!

"The blessings of the LORD brings ________, without painful toil for it." PROVERBS 10:22

It "grows as God causes it to grow." COLOSSIANS 2:19

"Night and day, whether he sleeps or gets up, the seed (investment money) sprouts and grows, though he does not know how." MARK 4:27

Just like a small acorn can grow into a mighty oak tree, so also the miracle of compound interest is able to grow our portfolio into a fully funded retirement plan.

"When you sow (________), you do not plant the body that will be, but just a seed...But God gives it a body as He has ________, and to each kind of seed He gives its own body." 1 CORINTHIANS 15:37-38

After years of investing, "You take out what you did not ________ and reap what you did not sow." LUKE 19:21

THIS IS ALL THE WORK OF GOD AND THE MIRACLE OF COMPOUNDING INTEREST!

"God has been making it grow." 1 CORINTHIANS 3:6

IMPORTANT: KEEP COSTS LOW

The expenses associated with operating a fund is the key driver of differences in fund performance. Keeping cost low is why investing in low cost index mutual funds should be the basis of your portfolio. The late Jack Bogle, the originator of the index mutual fund says, "In the mutual fund field, therefore, costs assume a tremendous importance for the long-term investor. Other things being equal, lower costs mean higher returns."

The late Jack Bogle would always say, "You get what you don't pay for."

"Teach me what I ________ see." JOB 34:32

INVEST IN BROAD BASED INDEX STOCK MUTUAL FUNDS

Instead of hiring a manager to actively select the stocks or bonds in your mutual fund portfolio, an index fund simply tracks a portion of the market. The most well known index fund is probably the S&P 500 Index, which tracks 500 of the largest stocks of the U.S. stock market.

For further diversification another solid choice would be the U.S. Total Stock Market Index Fund, which includes the stocks of the S&P 500, Mid-Cap and Small-Cap stocks of around 3000 to 4000 U.S. companies. These two broad market index funds give you instant diversification, a much smarter choice for the average investor, than trying to pick a few individual stocks. These Vanguard funds have razor thin expense ratios of 0.04%. Other fund families to consider are Fidelity, or Schwab.

Burton Malkiel says, "The index performance is not mediocre—it exceeds the results achieved by the typical active manager. And the results hold for big stocks and small, domestic as well as international. Moreover, the results are obtained if one looks at ten or twenty year results. And it works for the bond market as well as the stock market. Index investing is smart investing."

"He set my feet on a rock and gave me a firm place to stand." PSALM 40:2

"My feet stand on level ground." PSALM 26:12

"Teach me your way, LORD; lead me in a straight path." PSALM 27:11

THAT ROCK, LEVEL GROUND AND STRAIGHT PATH IN INVESTING IS LOW COST BROAD BASED INDEX MUTUAL FUNDS!

So be a patient long-term investor in a broad based, low cost, index mutual fund!

"Buy the truth and do not ________ it—wisdom, instruction and insight as well." PROVERBS 23:23

"Better one handful with ________________ than two handfuls with toil and chasing after the wind." ECCLESIASTES 4:6

"If you pay attention to the commands of the LORD your God that I give you this day and carefully follow them, you will always be at the _____, never at the ________." DEUTERONOMY 28:13

THE SIMPLEST WAY TO INVEST: TARGET DATE FUNDS

The simplest way for any investor to invest without requiring you to do anything but automate your investment dollars into the fund is to invest in a target date fund. Simply put, this is investing your retirement dollars into a fund of funds with a glide path to decrease the aggressiveness of the asset allocation as you approach retirement. The target date fund automatically rebalances the portfolio for you.

THE SMALL CAP AND VALUE PREMIUMS

Historical academic research has clearly shown that small cap stocks typically beat large cap stocks and value stocks typically outperform growth stocks over the long-term. If you are going to try to outperform the stock market index, I would choose to follow the academic research and invest in a small cap value mutual fund or ETF. If you choose to overweight your broad based index mutual fund with a small cap value fund/ETF, I would recommend you only direct 25% or less of your portfolio in this area.

MUTUAL FUNDS VS ETFs

As individual investors, if we don't have any particular insight about whether a specific stock is priced correctly or not, we can instead own hundreds, if not thousands, of stocks via a commingled investment vehicle such as an index mutual fund or ETF.

"You don't have to try to find the needle in the haystack, just buy the haystack." the late Jack Bogle, founder of Vanguard

For most investors they will be better served by investing in index mutual funds, especially if using Dollar-Cost-Averaging. The reason, ETFs are better for lump sum investing, and it is too tempting to use ETFs for frequent trading.

Burton Malkiel defines when best to use ETFs versus index mutual funds when he writes, "ETFs are an excellent vehicle for the investment of lump sums that are to be allocated to index funds. ETFs require the payment of transaction costs, however, including brokerage fees (some discount brokers offer commission free trading of ETFs) and bid-ask spreads. No-load index mutual funds will better serve investors who will be accumulating index shares over time in small amounts (as in Dollar-Cost-Averaging)."

TAX ADVANTAGE INVESTMENT VEHICLES: 401(k) or 403(b)

You should always use a tax-advantaged investment account before a taxable account, unless the money is to be used in the next few years. Why? You save in taxes on each dollar invested exactly the amount of your tax bracket.

These accounts are named for the area of the tax code that authorized their use. In the case of the 401(k) and 403(b), these accounts are invested pre-tax, meaning the dollars invested are subtracted from your taxable income and invested prior to you receiving your paycheck.

TAX ADVANTAGE INVESTMENT VEHICLES: TRADITIONAL IRA or ROTH IRA

The Traditional IRA works the same way as the 401(k) and 403(b) except the amount invested is limited to $7000 if your age is under fifty, and when fifty or older is given a $1000 catch-up provision for a total allowable investment of $8000 per year. Your best option if you have a long time horizon is probably using the Roth IRA. Money for the Roth IRA is invested after tax. In this case the dollar invested in theory is minus your current tax bracket (obviously we invest in full dollar amounts). The beauty of the Roth IRA is your money grows tax free, and is tax free upon withdrawal, can pass to heirs without them owing taxes, and is not subject to Required Minimum Distributions.

TAX ADVANTAGED INVESTMENT VEHICLE: 529 COLLEGE SAVINGS

For private school tuition or college savings I recommend the use of the tax-advantaged 529 Savings plan. Each state has their own 529 Savings plan, and you are not limited to using your own state plan. Go online at www.collegesavings.org to compare and evaluate different plans.

Jack Bogle writes, "By age 18, the stock/bond allocation should shift from 80/20 to 35/65." When college expenses come due, you can sell stocks for tuition in the good stock return years, and sell bonds in the poor stock return years.

THE BEST INVESTMENT METHOD: DOLLAR-COST-AVERAGING

Jonathan Clements says, "Dollar-Cost-Averaging is a disciplined, no nonsense strategy of investing the same sum of money every paycheck no matter how the market is performing. It helps us to overcome our reluctance to invest during market declines."

Burton Malkiel says, "It seems only logical that making many investments in the stock market at periodic intervals—known as dollar-cost-averaging—will provide greater stability of return than a single all at once commitment. The reason is that a large single investment determines, for once and for all, the price at which you have committed your assets."

"Whoever gathers money [illegible] by [illegible] makes it grow." PROVERBS 13:11

TRACKING YOUR INVESTMENTS

As a long-term investor there is no need to track the market or the direction of your investments more than a couple of times per year.

I recommend using the Boldin Retirement Planner calculator to evaluate, once per year, if you are on track to reach your long-term goals.

"A person's wisdom yields patience." PROVERBS 19:11

"May the God who gives [illegible] and encouragement give you the same attitude of mind…." ROMANS 15:5

TIME HORIZON

Your Time Horizon is the time in years from when you start investing for a goal until the time when you'll need the money. You must remember to consider your personal investment time horizon when you start the investing process. Hopefully, if you are using the wisdom I'm presenting as your guide, your time horizon for investing in stocks is somewhere between five and fifty plus years.

INVESTING PATIENCE

Your investing mindset is going to be one of patience. If you do your job, which is to build your investment money up to at least 15% of your gross income, and start investing early with your first full-time job in your twenties, you have an excellent chance to reach your long-term goals and become financially (in)dependent.

"But hope that is seen is no hope at all. Who ________ for what they already have? But if we hope for what we do not have, we ________ patiently." ROMANS 8:24-25

"Whoever is patient has great understanding." PROVERBS 14:29

"This calls for ________ endurance and faithfulness on the part of God's people." REVELATION 13:10

BE CAREFUL OF THE INVESTING ADVICE YOU LISTEN TO AND ACT ON

As Warren Buffett once said, "Be fearful when others are greedy, and greedy when others are fearful."

"By your wisdom and ________ you have gained wealth for yourself and amassed gold and silver in your treasuries." EZEKIEL 28:4

"If you are wise, your wisdom will reward you." PROVERBS 9:12

FINANCIAL (IN)DEPENDENCE ON GOD

"So you must be careful to do ________ they tell you." MATTHEW 23:3

"Success, success to you, and success to those who help you, for your ________ will help you." 1 CHRONICLES 12:18

"Now what I am commanding you today is not too ________ for you or beyond your reach. DEUTERONOMY 30:11

"All of us, then, who are mature should take such a view of things. And if, on some point you think ________, that too God will make clear to you." PHILIPPIANS 3:15

CONCLUSION

Investing is putting money to work for the long-term, so that when it is needed in the future you will have gained a real return on your money greater than the inflation rate. When it comes to investing with increased rewards (returns) there is always increased risk, as higher investment returns are compensation for the additional risk you are taking. The primary assets of investing include stocks, bonds, REIT's, and cash (mostly as held in an emergency fund). Stock investing is buying a stake in a company or corporation, with the hope of receiving future value through company growth and dividend payouts. Bonds are a way individual investors can loan money to the U.S. Treasury or individual corporations, with the expectation of receiving your principal investment in return with agreed upon interest payments, over a specified period. REITs (Real Estate Investment Trusts) Index Mutual Funds allow the hands off investor to gain access to the benefits of real estate by participating in the dividends gained through the fund, which are required to be paid out, from the rental/lease agreements they have under contract.

Focus your investing energy on the things you can control. Having a comprehensive financial plan, your savings rate, your asset allocation, minimizing investment costs, understanding your risk tolerance, using tax advantage investment vehicles, and making level headed decisions. The miracle of compound interest combined with time in the stock market produces investing results. Index mutual funds should be the foundation of every investment portfolio. A first time fund owner should choose either the S&P 500 Index or the U.S. Total Stock Market Index fund as their initial investment choice for diversification and a low expense ratio. Target Date Funds are the simplest way to invest and get instant diversification and age appropriate asset allocation. ETFs are best for lump sum investments, while index mutual funds are best for investing small sums on a regular basis as in Dollar-Cost-Averaging.

ACTION STEPS

1. Are you currently investing 15% of your salary in a tax advantaged savings plan at work or in a Roth IRA?

If not, contribute at least the minimum to get the company match in your 401(k), and add 1-2% each year as you receive raises from your employer.

2. Are you using index funds and dollar-cost-averaging your investment dollars?

If not, make index mutual funds the foundation of your investing, and automate your investing through dollar-cost-averaging.

3. Do you have a resilient and patient constitution, and desire to take advantage of the small cap and value stock premium?

Add a small cap value ETF of 10-25% to your current portfolio.

4. Are you using your investment dollars on legitimate investments such as stocks, bonds and REITs, or are you speculating in cryptocurrency or other speculative commodities?

At least 90% of your investing dollars should be concentrated in legitimate investments, with less than 10% in speculative assets (and I use the term "assets" loosely).

LESSON 9

UNDERSTANDING THE STOCK MARKET

"He (God) does as He pleases with the powers of heaven and the peoples of the earth."
DANIEL 4:35

"I have seen something else under the sun: The race is not to the swift or the battle to the strong, nor does food come to the wise or wealth to the brilliant or favor to the learned; but time and chance happen to them all."
ECCLESIASTES 9:11

THE HISTORY OF THE STOCK MARKET

History cannot predict the future, but history often will repeat itself if we do not learn from the actions of the past.

"Ask the former __________ and find out what their ancestors learned." JOB 8:8

"This is what the LORD says: 'Stand at the crossroads and look; ask for the ancient paths, ask where the __________ __________ is, and walk in it, and you will find rest for your souls.'" JEREMIAH 6:16

"What has been will be __________, and what has been done will be __________ again; there is nothing new under the sun." ECCLESIASTES 1:9

William J. Bernstein says, "As an investor, it is more rewarding to study investment history than to study the present market activity or estimates of the future. Visit your local library and read the financial section of your favorite…newspaper for 1928-1929, 1957,1962, 1973, 1987, 2000, and 2008…. Every market is different in the details. But major characteristics of markets are remarkably similar, time after time."

The first thing one must understand about the stock market is that it is CYCLICAL. It can go up or down at any time, and we must learn not to overreact to such stock market developments or we may cause irreparable harm to our investment portfolio.

J David Stein writes, "Market participants could collectively drive security prices to levels well beyond reasonable expectations. In other words, the combination of investors' greed and their fear of missing out was so powerful at times that they were willing to pay exorbitant sums for expected cash flow growth. During other periods, fear of losses caused investors to dump assets indiscriminately, pushing values well below historical averages."

This "irrational exuberance" as coined by the Federal Reserve Chairman Alan Greenspan during the build up of the Dot.com Bubble of 2000 would soon burst and everyone in the stock market at the time felt the pain of a sudden and extreme decline. These kinds of market events are often referred to as the GREED / FEAR CYCLE.

The most important thing for the average investor during these times of steep declines is to NOT PANIC, AND TO CONTINUE TO BUY SHARES AT SALE PRICES through regular investing using index mutual funds and the method of dollar-cost-averaging. Then as the market recovers, your portfolio will also recover. A permanent loss is inevitable, if the market decline has scared you into selling, and scared you to the point you are afraid to re-enter the market.

THE STOCK MARKET IS CYCLICAL

The entire point of this lesson is to help you understand the cyclical nature of the stock market, the volatility that comes from investing in stocks, and to expect significant market downturns.

Truth teller Ben Carlson writes, "The U.S. stock market has experienced a double digit correction once every year-and-a-half or so and a bear market once every four years on average."

Charles D. Ellis explains, "Investors who were particularly enamored of Internet stocks (in the 2000 Dot.com Bubble) were chanting the mantra of all stock market bubbles: 'This time is different.'" If you hear or read that statement in your investment lifetime, immediately decrease your aggressive growth stock allocation and wait for the bubble to burst, before again diversifying your stock allocation.

HISTORICAL MARKET DECLINES

"Do not tremble, do not be afraid. Did I not proclaim this and   it long ago? You are my witnesses." ISAIAH 44:8

"Command those who are rich in this present world not to be arrogant nor to put their   in wealth, which is so uncertain, but to put their hope in   , who richly provides us with everything for our enjoyment." 1 TIMOTHY 6:17

THE RETURNS OF STOCKS AND OTHER INVESTMENTS

Since 1926 large stocks have returned an average of 10% per year.

Since 1926 long-term government bonds have returned between 5-6%

Money market mutual funds usually earn interest between 1 and 3% per year.

The S&P 500 averages ~10% return with a SD of ~15%, with returns falling within one Standard Deviation 68% of the time.

Long-term corporate bonds average ~6.4% return with a SD of 8.4%.

Long-term government bonds average 5.8% with SD of 9.3%.

The Standard Deviation of stocks is a measure of stock market volatility or risk.

"Remember this, keep it in mind, take it to heart." ISAIAH 46:8

THE STOCK MARKET: A RANDOM WALK

The Random Walk Theory basically says there is no real time way of telling which direction the stock market is going to turn.

Burton G. Malkiel in his classic book "A Random Walk Down Wall Street" says, "The results reveal that past movements in stock prices cannot be used reliably to foretell future movements." "This is what economists mean when they say that stock prices behave very much like a random walk." "The history of stock price movements contains no useful information that will enable an investor consistently to out perform a buy-and-hold strategy in managing a portfolio."

"Since ______ knows the future, who can tell someone else what is to come?" ECCLESIASTES 8:7

"NO ONE can comprehend what goes on under the sun. Despite all their efforts to search it out, no one can ______ its meaning. Even if the wise claim they know, they cannot really ______ it." ECCLESIASTES 8:17

"Who then is like Me? Let him proclaim it. Let him declare and lay out before Me what has happened since… and what is ______—yes, let them foretell what will come." ISAIAH 44:7

"I said, 'Sovereign LORD, You alone know." EZEKIEL 37:3

THE GREED VS FEAR CYCLES

When investing you should not find yourself getting caught up in the irrational exuberance of the greed cycle, meaning you are adding additional money to your stock investments because the market is climbing, rather than simply dollar-cost-averaging.

"The greedy bring ______ to their households." PROVERBS 15:17

"Before a ______ the heart is haughty, but humility comes before honor." PROVERBS 18:12

"She sees that her trading is profitable, and her lamp does not ______ at night." PROVERBS 31:18

I DO NOT WANT YOU TO SUCCUMB TO THE SIN OF THE FEAR CYCLE AND SELL STOCKS ON THE WAY DOWN OR NEAR THE BOTTOM!

"'Testing will ______ come'...declares the Sovereign LORD." EZEKIEL 21:13

"In their peril their courage ______ away." PSALM 107:26

"Hearts melt, knees give way, bodies tremble, every face grows pale." NAHUM 2:10

There will be times of a sudden stock market collapse!

"Woe to you…where all who…became rich through her wealth! In ______ she has been brought to ruin!" REVELATION 18:19

A paper loss is not a true capital loss until you sell at the bottom.

"Cast but a glance at riches, and they are ________, for they will surely sprout wings and fly off." **PROVERBS 23:5**

If you find yourself in a down market with too high a stock allocation, DON'T CHOOSE TO SELL AT THE BOTTOM! If you do:

"The wealth they ________ is gone." **JEREMIAH 48:46**

"Surely I have acted like a ________ and have been terribly wrong." **1 SAMUEL 26:21**

THE STOCK MARKET WILL RECOVER

Believe that every bear market will end, just as all bear markets eventually end. Believe there are more embedded positive surprises in asset classes purchased during periods of fear than there are negative surprises.

"Though I have fallen, I will ________." **MICAH 7:8**

"Then you will know that I am the LORD: those who ________ Me will not be disappointed." **ISAIAH 49:23**

"When times are good, be happy; but when times are bad, consider this: God has made the one ________ the other. Therefore, no one can discover anything about their future." **ECCLESIASTES 7:14**

COMFORT FROM GOD'S WORD IN A DECLINING MARKET

"Is ________ too hard for the LORD?" **GENESIS 18:14**

"Do not be afraid. Stand ________ and you will see the deliverance the LORD will bring you today. **EXODUS 14:13**

"Commit your way to the LORD; ________ in Him and He will do this." **PSALM 37:5**

"Since ancient times no one has heard, no ear perceived, no eye has seen any God besides You, who acts ________ of those who wait for Him." **ISAIAH 64:4**

"They will have no fear of bad news; their hearts are ________, trusting in the LORD. Their hearts are secure, they will have no fear." **PSALM 112:7-8**

THE STOCK MARKET WILL RECOVER

"'You of little faith,' He (Jesus) said, 'Why did you ________.'" **MATTHEW 14:31**

"Now then, ________ ________ and see this great thing the LORD is about to do before your eyes!" 1 SAMUEL 12:16

"I ________ restore their fortunes, declares the LORD." JEREMIAH 32:44

"And will make you prosper ________ than before. Then you will know that I am the LORD." EZEKIEL 36:11

"For I will ________ their fortunes and have compassion on them." JEREMIAH 33:26

CONCLUSION

History cannot predict the future, but history will often repeat itself if we do not learn from the actions of the past. The stock market is cyclical, and goes up or down at any time, and we must learn not to overreact to such stock market developments or we may cause irreparable harm to our investment portfolio. Dollar-Cost-Averaging your investments is the best way to continue to invest for the average investor during all market conditions. When the market is going down you are buying more shares of stocks at a lower cost. The best indicator of your risk tolerance is how you responded during a severe market decline of 30-50%. The direction of the stock market is said to be a "random walk" and cannot be accurately predicted by anyone repeatedly in advance. A paper loss in the market is not a true capital loss until you sell at or near the bottom.

ACTION STEPS

1. Have you lived through a stock market decline of 50% or greater? How did you respond?

If you have previously sold out of the stock market during a steep decline, resolve to never do it again through the strength of God's Word as recorded earlier!

2. Your response in a stock market's steep decline is the best indicator of your personal risk tolerance. Based on your past behavior during market downturns how would you grade your personal risk tolerance?

If you learned from past market declines you have average or poor risk tolerance, adjust your asset allocation until you can sleep well. Re-read the above scriptures until your faith allows you to continue to dollar-cost-average through the next decline, or hire an advisor who can talk you off the cliff during the next market downturn.

LESSON 10

ASSET ALLOCATION AND DIVERSIFICATION

"But divide your investments among many places,
for you do not know what risks might lie ahead."
ECCLESIASTES 11:2 NLT

"For you do not know which will succeed, whether this or that,
or whether both will do equally well."
ECCLESIASTES 11:6

DIVERSIFICATION

This is what you get by investing in broad based stock mutual funds / ETFs or bond mutual funds / ETFs. You automatically own a diverse portfolio of stocks or bonds, instead of having the risk of owning a few individual stocks or bonds. Broad diversification gives your portfolio a measure of safety, as you own many stocks to buffer the occasional failure of a given company, and because in the words of the late Jack Bogle, "you buy the haystack," instead of having to try to pick the winning stocks.

TARGET DATE FUNDS: THE IMPORTANCE OF ASSET ALLOCATION

Deciding on an appropriate Asset Allocation with appropriate diversification is the most important investment decision you make! Why? Greater than 90% of your return on investments is based solely on your asset allocation.

If you don't believe me, then open your newspaper that tracks mutual funds, and look at the Target Dated Mutual Fund returns from a couple of different fund families. These funds will be identified by a date that is supposed to coincide closely with your date of expected retirement. What you will notice, if we are in a bull market (meaning the stock market is making gains) is that the dated funds further out have higher returns than those close to the date you are looking at the returns. You should even see incremental change in the returns of these funds. Why? The answer is plain and simply due to Asset Allocation, the amount of stocks vs bonds held in each fund. The funds dated closer to the date you are looking, will be invested more conservatively with a larger portion of bonds. The funds dated far away from the current date are going to have the highest stock allocation making them more aggressive, with higher returns in a bull market.

ACTUAL TARGET DATE FUND YTD EARNINGS FROM DECEMBER 30, 2023 FOR THREE FUND FAMILIES—THE STAR TRIBUNE

VANGUARD		FIDELITY	T. ROWE PRICE
2020 FUND	13.2%	12.4%	13.1%
2025 FUND	15.5%	13.6%	14.2%
2030 FUND	17.1%	14.8%	15.9%
2035 FUND	18.3%	17.1%	17.6%
2040 FUND	19.7%	19.4%	19.0%
2045 FUND	21.0%	20.0%	19.9%
2050 FUND	21.7%	19.9%	20.2%

What you are looking at above is the actual yearly returns of Target Date Funds from three fund families: Vanguard, Fidelity, and T. Rowe Price for 2023. What you should notice is what I described before this chart for a rising market. The later dated funds incrementally have higher returns due to having a greater allocation of stocks to bonds, thus the 2050 funds have higher returns than the 2045 funds, 2045 funds have >returns than 2040 funds, and so on (with the one Fidelity exception). The numbers for each of the funds is not the same because each fund family has its own proprietary formula for the glide path of their funds.

THE FORMULA FOR DETERMINING STOCK VS BOND ASSET ALLOCATION

The formula that is most often cited for the individual investor to determine their stock vs bond allocation is: 100 minus your age=the % of money you should place in stocks. Using the example of a 20 year old, we take 100-20=80% in stocks and 20% in bonds. An example using a 70 year old, we take 100-70=30% in stocks and 70% in bonds. With today's significant increase in life expectancy and improved health care, I personally believe this is a bit conservative making it more likely that you will run out of money at the end of life.

For investors with moderate risk tolerance, I would recommend using 110-age=stock allocation, and for the highly risk tolerant individuals I would probably recommend 120-age=stock allocation.

Then the LORD said, "My spirit will not contend with humans forever, for they are mortal; their days will be a hundred and twenty years." GENESIS 6:3

Now don't place yourself in the high risk tolerant category until you have lived through a steep market decline and were able to maintain your fortitude, continuing to invest in stocks on the way down, at the bottom, and on the way back up. By a steep decline, I am referring to 30-50% declines as occurred in 2000-2001 and 2008-2009 both of which shed 50% for stock funds requiring a full 100% rebound to get back to even.

ASSET ALLOCATION IS THE #1 DRIVER OF PORTFOLIO RETURNS

The late Jack Bogle writes, "The most fundamental decision of investing is the allocation of your assets... According to a recent study, that decision has accounted for an astounding 94% of the difference in total returns...The 94% figure suggests that long-term fund investors might profit by concentrating more on allocation of their investments between stock and bond funds and less on the question of which particular stock and bond funds to hold."

"For you do not know which will ________, whether this or that (stocks or bonds), or whether both will do equally well." ECCLESIASTES 11:6

"But divide your investments among ________ places, for you do not know what risks might lie ahead." ECCLESIASTES 11:2

William J. Bernstein in "The Intelligent Asset Allocator" asks a very important question, "So how do you arrive at the allocation that will provide the most return with the least amount of risk? You can't. But don't feel bad, because neither can anybody else." "One of the fundamental laws of investing: in the long run you are compensated for bearing risk. Conversely, if you seek safety, your returns will be low. Experienced investors understand that reward and risk are inextricably intertwined; one of the most reliable ways to spot fraud is the promise of excessive returns with low risk."

"When you lie down, you will not be afraid; when you lie down, your ________ will be sweet. Have no fear of sudden disaster or of the ________ that overtakes the wicked." PROVERBS 3:24-25

William J. Bernstein says, "Dividing your portfolio between assets with uncorrelated results increases return while decreasing risk." "The point cannot be stated strongly enough: mixing assets with uncorrelated returns reduces risk, because when one of the assets is zigging, it is likely the other is zagging." "Sticking by your asset allocation policy through thick and thin is much more important than picking the 'best' allocation." "The essence of effective portfolio construction is the use of a large number of poorly correlated assets."

"The Word of the LORD to them will become: Do this, do that, a rule for this, a rule for that, a ________ here, a ________ there...." ISAIAH 28:13

"The key to success in investing is to invest with the asset mix that's best for you considering:

- Your financial situation: assets, income, and savings—now and in the future
- Your age
- Your emotional strengths—particularly at market highs and lows—and your attitude toward market risk
- Your knowledge of and interest in investing"

"Know thyself and match your investing to who you are and where you are in life."
—BURTON MALKIEL AND CHARLES D. ELLIS

Charles D. Ellis in his classic book "Winning the Loser's Game: Timeless Strategies for Successful Investing" writes, "Experienced investors understand four powerful truths about investing, and wise investors will govern their investing by adhering to them:

1. The dominating reality of investing is that the most important decision is your long-term mix of assets: how much in stocks, real estate, bonds, or cash.
2. That asset mix should be determined partly by your real purpose for the money, partly by when the money will be used, and partly by your ability to stay the course.
3. Diversify within each asset class and among asset classes. Bad things do happen—usually as surprises.
4. Be patient and persistent. Good things come in spurts—usually when least expected —and fidgety investors fare badly. 'Plan your play and play your plan,' say the great coaches, and that takes you back to number 1."

REBALANCING

William J. Bernstein says, "An important assumption underlies all of the portfolio discussions thus far: that at the end of the year the investor rebalances the portfolio back to the target compositions. If a particular asset has done extraordinarily well, its portfolio weighting will increase; consequently, enough of it must be sold and reinvested in the poorly performing assets, to return to the target composition (policy allocation)." "In practical terms, this means rebalancing no more than once per year."

"The wise heart will know the time and procedure. For there is a proper time and for every matter." ECCLESIASTES 8:5-6

Burton Malkiel and Charles Ellis write, "Rebalancing reduces the volatility and riskiness of your investment portfolio and can often enhance your returns." "Rebalancing simply involves periodically checking the allocation of the different types of investments in your portfolio and bringing them back to the desired percentages." "It involves not letting the asset proportions in your portfolio stray too far from the ideal you have chosen as best for you." "Investors who rebalance their portfolio in a disciplined way are well rewarded." "Rebalancing will not always increase returns. But it will always reduce the riskiness of the portfolio and it will always ensure that your actual allocation stays consistent with the right allocation for your needs and temperament."

"Whoever fears God will avoid extremes." ECCLESIASTES 7:18

"The horse (asset allocation) is made ready for battle (down market), but victory (financial success) rests with the LORD." PROVERBS 21:3

MODEL PORTFOLIOS

MERRIMAN FINANCIAL EDUCATION FOUNDATION

Worldwide Ultimate Buy and Hold Portfolio
S&P 500 10%, US Large Cap Value 10%, US Small Cap Blend 10%, US Small Cap Value 10%, REIT 10%, Int Large Cap Blend 10%, Int Large Cap Value 10%, Int Small Cap Blend 10%, Int Small Cap Value 10%, EmMrkt 10%

U.S. Four Funds Portfolio
S & P 500 (Large Cap Blend) 25%, Large Cap Value 25%, Small Cap Blend 25%, Small Cap Value 25%

Chris Pedersen Two Funds For Life Portfolio
Target Date Fund 80-90% Small Cap Value ETF 20%-10%

BOGLEHEAD THREE FUND PORTFOLIO

Vanguard Total Stock Market Index Fund	60%
Vanguard International Stock Market Index Fund	20%
Vanguard Total Bond Market Index Fund	20%

BURTON MALKIEL'S ALLOCATION RANGES BY AGE GROUP

Age Group	Percent in Stocks	Percent in Bonds
20-30s	75-90	25-10
40-50s	65-75	35-25
60s	45-65	55-35
70s	35-50	65-50
80s	20-40	80-60

CHARLES ELLIS' ALLOCATION RANGES BY AGE GROUP

Age Group	Percent in Stocks	Percent in Bonds
20-30s	100	0
40s	90-100	10-0
50s	75-85	25-15
60s	70-80	30-20
70s	40-60	60-40
80s and beyond	30-50	70-50

CONCLUSION

Target Date funds are designed as stand alone funds with an asset allocation and glide path appropriate for your chosen or anticipated retirement date. Asset allocation is something an investor can control and is the number one driver of portfolio returns. It accounts for ~94% of portfolio return. International stocks belong in everyone's portfolio, as the United States represents less than half of the world's economic activity and stock market capitalization. You should rebalance your asset allocation at least once per year or anytime your asset allocation diverges from your desired allocation by more than 5-10%. Optimal investment strategies must be age related, appropriate to your risk tolerance and investing time horizon.

ACTION STEPS

1. Do you know the current asset allocation for your investment portfolio? Is it appropriate for your age, risk tolerance and time horizon?

If you don't immediately know the answer to these questions, research your current asset allocation using tools provided by your brokerage or fund family. If you're using an advisor that is doing this for you, give them a call and ask the same questions.

2. When was the last time you rebalanced your portfolio?

Do you own a Target Date Fund or have an advisor that is doing this for you?

3. How many uncorrelated assets or income drivers do you have as part of your portfolio?

LESSON 11

HAVING A GOD HONORING FINANCIAL PLAN

"Commit to the LORD whatever you do,
and He will establish your plans."
PROVERBS 16:3

"He will teach us His ways,
so that we may walk in His paths."
ISAIAH 2:3 / MICAH 4:2

"Now this is what the LORD Almighty says:
'Give careful thought to your ways.'"
HAGGAI 1:5 / HAGGAI 1:7

PLACE GOD IN THE HEART OF YOUR FINANCIAL PLAN

"Those who trust in ______________ are fools, but those who walk in ______________ are kept safe." PROVERBS 28:26

"Show me Your ________, LORD, teach me Your ________." PSALM 25:4

"Trust in the LORD with ______________ heart and lean not on your own understanding; in all your ways ______________ to Him, and He will make your paths ______________." PROVERBS 3:5-6

"The plan of the Holy One…let it approach, let it come into ________, so we may ________ it." ISAIAH 5:19

"In their hearts humans ______________ their course, but the LORD establishes their ______________." PROVERBS 16:9

WORK CLOSELY WITH YOUR SPOUSE: DESIGN / IMPLEMENT YOUR PLAN

You have three members of your financial dream team, you, your spouse, and God. You want all three to be on the same page.

"Though one may be overpowered, ________ can defend themselves. A cord of three strands is not quickly broken." ECCLESIASTES 4:12

"They will make your load lighter, because they will ______________ it with you." EXODUS 18:22

Working with your spouse and being unified in your financial plan is the only way to success. As Jesus says in Matthew 12:25 or Mark 3:25,

"Every...household ______ against itself will not stand." MATTHEW 12:25

KNOW YOUR SAVING GOAL

You don't need a specific ______ to save, but there are a lot of easy reasons: like an emergency fund, your retirement, your child's college education, a down payment on a home, for buying your next used car, replacing an appliance, or gaining control of your time, just to name a few.

Morgan Housel in "The Psychology of Money: Timeless Lessons on Wealth, Greed, and Happiness" writes, "Do not aim to be coldly ______ when making financial decisions... ______ is more realistic and you have a better chance of sticking with it for the long run, which is what matters most when managing money." "Long-term financial planning is ______. But things change—both the world around you, and your own goals and desires." "Independence has always been my personal financial goal." "I mostly just want to wake up every day knowing my family and I can do whatever we want to do on our own terms. Every financial decision we make revolves around that goal."

IMPLEMENT YOUR PLAN WITH DILIGENCE, INTENTIONALITY AND WISDOM

"A discerning person keeps ______ in view." PROVERBS 17:24

"The desires of the ______ are fully satisfied." PROVERBS 13:20

"For ______ is protection just as money is protection. But the advantage of ______ is that wisdom preserves the lives of its possessors." ECCLESIASTES 7:12 NASB

"My son, do not let wisdom and ______ out of your sight, preserve sound ______ and discretion." PROVERBS 3:21

"But wisdom is proved ______ by her actions." MATTHEW 11:19

SENSIBLE MONEY MANAGEMENT

Jonathan Clements in "The Little Book of Main Street Money" says, "Markets are rational, but humans are not. Sensible money management is pretty ______: Keep debt low, save regularly, have an emergency fund, hold down costs, buy a few broad based mutual funds, control risk through asset allocation, and hold down taxes. Before you make any financial decisions you should consider a number of factors to include: Your risk tolerance, your goals, your income, the size of your nest egg, and your tax bracket. Our ______ should focus on things we can control. We can't control the inflation rate, bond yields, and the direction of the stock market. But we can control how we ______ and save, how much we pay in investment ______ and taxes, how much investment ______ we take on by diversification and asset allocation, and how we react to market highs and market lows. Every financial decision comes with a tradeoff. Within reason our financial choices aren't bad if they match our values, but they are indeed choices."

The late Jack Bogle writes, "When it comes to investing, the ______ invested, the length of ______ that an investment is made, in conjunction with the rate of ______ that it earns, ultimately determines your wealth accumulation. It is impossible to overstate the critical role of ______ to decrease investment risk in an intelligent investment program. Intelligent investors try to separate emotion from reason, and trust in reason to prevail over the long term."

William J. Bernstein asks, "Will you be able to self direct your financial life, or will you need the help of an advisor? The only real guidance you'll need is in two distinct areas: (1) Your asset allocation, and (2) Your self discipline. If you have a firm handle on your ______ tolerance you are well on your way to self directing."

A WRITTEN FINANCIAL PLAN AND INVESTMENT POLICY STATEMENT

Having a written Financial Plan or an Investment Policy Statement may help you become ______ times wealthier than the average saver for retirement without a written plan, according to Paul Merriman, founder of the Merriman Financial Education Foundation. Only 35 percent of retirees have a written plan for their future finances...Those who ______ to plan, plan to fail.

Kathleen Coxwell writes, "An IPS is a document that is meant to define:

1) Your goals for your investments
2) Strategies for achieving those objectives
3) A framework for making intelligent changes to your investments
4) Options for what to do if things don't go as expected.

INVESTMENT POLICY STATEMENT

Ben Carlson writes, "The Investment Policy Statement is where you write down all of your do's and don'ts, your if/then statements, and your ______ and objectives. It's your plan of attack that ______ your actions." It's "a written document that outlines how you would like to implement your portfolio and maintain it over time." "Passive, systematic, ______ investment strategies are the best option for a majority of investors...You...have a higher probability of success with index funds and ETFs than you do by trying to choose the small number of active funds that consistently outperform."

Ben Carlson in "A Wealth of Common Sense: Why Simplicity Trumps Complexity in Any Investment Plan" writes, "An investment philosophy is simply a set of ______ that will guide your actions when making portfolio decisions. It's your core beliefs." "If you want to be a successful investor, the first step involves defining your core beliefs...These beliefs should ______ all subsequent portfolio management decisions." "Your investment plan should be designed specifically for the end user—you... build the one you ______ you will follow. You have to be brutally honest with yourself about your ability to handle risk." "Nothing is permanent until you make it so...You can make minor changes along the way if you determine, after a cycle of fear and greed, that you don't have the right asset allocation in place."

YOUR FINANCIAL PLAN / INVESTMENT POLICY STATEMENT INCLUDES:

"Identifying your resources, needs, and goals
Assessing your time horizon for each financial goal
Understanding your risk tolerance and having a plan for market crashes
Establish an age appropriate asset allocation and modify to more bonds as you approach the time the money is to be used
How often you will check your portfolio and what tools you will use
How often you will rebalance your portfolio."

A GOD HONORING FINANCIAL PLAN WILL ADDRESS:

How we go about our work.
How we are stewards of God's gifts.
How we are going to determine our offering to the Lord.
How we are going to track our monthly cash flow.
How we are going to address our debt.
What our financial goals are, and how we're, with the help of God going to meet them.
What types of investment vehicles and funds are we going to use for our investments.
What types of insurance coverage are we going to have?

A COMPREHENSIVE INVESTMENT PLAN

Ben Carlson writes, "For investors it all comes down to creating a comprehensive investment plan. Your plan should include…your investment philosophy, asset allocation, a rebalancing schedule, what kinds of ________ you will or won't make, and so on…A plan allows you to utilize a portfolio to control your behavior to achieve your financial objectives." "There is a sure way to fail—never implement a ________ in the first place." "Since successful investing comes down more to your ________ than your actions, preparing yourself for anything is the best form of planning." "It's the repetition of good ________ that leads to favorable outcomes over time. Good investors have a high tolerance for repetition, even when it requires doing nothing over and over again."

Charles D. Ellis writes, "Getting it right on investment policy, with or without a professional advisor, is up to ________ the investor. After all, it is your money. You know the ________ about your overall financial and investment situation: Your earning power, your ability to save, when you plan to retire, your obligations for your children's educational expenses, the likely timing and scale of needs for spendable funds, and how you feel about the disciplines of investing. Only you can know your own ________ for changes in market prices, particularly at market extremes, when the pressures for change are the strongest. So it's your responsibility to know who you really are as an ________ and what you really want."

PLAN FOR WHEN THINGS DON'T GO ACCORDING TO PLAN

Morgan Housel says, "Planning is important, but the most important part of every plan, is to plan on the plan not going to plan." "A plan is only useful if it can survive . As a future filled with unknowns is everyone's reality." "The idea that a things account for most results is not just true for companies in your investment portfolio. It's also an important part of your own behavior as an investor."

A GOD HONORING FINANCIAL PLAN

In order for your financial plan to succeed you must execute the plan with diligence, and trust God to bless your plan.

"We want each of you to show this same to the very end, so that what you hope for may be fully realized." HEBREWS 6:11

"You need to so that when you have done the will of God, you will receive what He has promised." HEBREWS 10:36

"The LORD works out to its proper end." PROVERBS 16:4

"This is what the LORD says:...I will give them all the I have promised them." JEREMIAH 32:42

Financial (In)dependence = "Their prosperity is not in their own hands." JOB 21:16

CONCLUSION

Place God in the heart of your financial plan. Work closely with your spouse to design and implement your financial plan. Know your saving goals. By knowing your goal and the time horizon of the need for the money, you can make a wise choice in what type of savings or investing vehicle to use. We must implement our financial plan with diligence, intentionality, wisdom and discernment. Jonathan Clements writes: "Sensible money management is pretty straightforward: Keep debt low, save regularly, have an emergency fund, hold down costs, buy a few broad based mutual funds, control risk through asset allocation, and hold down taxes." While Paul Merriman says, "Having a written Financial Plan or an Investment Policy Statement may help you become five times wealthier than the average saver for retirement without a written plan." God is at the heart of the faithful fulfilling of any financial plan, what I call Financial (In)dependence. "Their prosperity is not in their own hands." JOB 21:16

ACTION STEPS

1. Do you have a written financial plan?

If not, work with your spouse over the next couple of weeks to write and define your family financial plan. If you already have a written financial plan, sit down and re-read it, and make any changes that are suitable.

2. When you write your personal family financial plan use the information provided to refine and direct your plan.

If you are working with an advisor, some of your financial plan probably should be done in conjunction with your advisor, or at least be used to judge the effectiveness of your advisor's advice and actions.

THE RON D. & SELENA J. FISCHER
GOD HONORING FINANCIAL PLAN

"Commit to the LORD whatever you do,
and He will establish your plans."
PROVERBS 16:3

"He will teach us His ways,
so that we may walk in His paths."
ISAIAH 2:3 & MICAH 4:2

Guiding Statement: We will seek to honor God in every aspect of our financial lives.

We will, with the help of God, maintain integrity in all financial matters.

We will, with the help of God, pay all bills on time.

We will, with the help of God, work faithfully in our jobs, always perform at our best, as if working for the Lord in everything we do.

We will, with the help of God, be mindful in our spending and good stewards of all of God's gifts.

We will, with the help of God, tithe our place of worship by giving an offering of 10% of our take home earnings, in thankfulness to God for all His blessings to us.

We will, with the help of God, use the difference between a gross pay tithe, and the net pay tithe, in ministries outside our congregation, and to lift up the poor.

We will, with the help of God, buy used, shop sales, use coupons, and not be concerned about name brands or what others think.

We will, with the help of God, use a budget to track our earnings, spending, and saving patterns until we are disciplined enough to meet all our financial goals.

We will, with the help of God, resolve to live debt free by:
Not carrying any credit card or revolving debt without full payment each month.
Paying cash for all large purchases, by saving in advance.
We will pay off our mortgage early, and own our home outright.

We will, with the help of God, redeem credit card points as they become available for cash.

We will, with the help of God, complete home maintenance and improvement projects that are within our abilities, on our own.

We will, with the help of God, save for large home improvement projects, get a few quotes, research the integrity of the companies bidding to do the work and manufacturers before moving forward with large expenditures.

We will, with the help of God, find a local trustworthy mechanic for vehicle maintenance and repairs.

We will, with the help of God, drive the same used vehicle, for the entirety of its useful life, striving for 8-15 years.

We will, with the help of God, establish an emergency fund with 6 months worth of monthly expenses.

We will, with the help of God, invest for Long-Term Goals of Retirement and College Savings:

> We will make retirement savings our first priority, investing 15% of our income.
>
> We will strive to reach a goal of 10-12 times our annual salaries at retirement
>
> We will make broad based index mutual funds the foundation of our retirement investing.
>
> We will strive to keep our investing costs low.
>
> We will use Tax Advantage Savings Plans including workplace 401(k) plans, IRA's, and Roth IRA's to help maximize our savings and minimize tax consequences
>
> We will Dollar-Cost-Average our investment dollars into all investment accounts and automate this savings in order to keep us on track in our investing.
>
> We will NOT sell stocks during a market decline, but continue to trust God and Dollar-Cost-Average our investment dollars in order to buy more stocks while on sale.
>
> We will only make portfolio changes THAT EITHER IMPROVE RETURNS OR DECREASE THE RISK OF OUR PORTFOLIO
>
> We will strive to save enough in our retirement savings to cover the eventuality of health care costs, and possibility of having to self-insure Long-Term Care costs.
>
> We will invest for our child's college education using a 529 Tax Advantaged Saving Plan.
>
> We will use a 529 College Savings Plan that is based on low cost index mutual funds.
>
> We will automate our savings into the 529 Plan keeping us on track for college savings.

We will, with the help of God, diversify our investments, and maintain an asset allocation appropriate for our investment Time Horizons, using domestic stock mutual funds, international stock mutual funds, bond mutual funds, and REIT Index funds.

We will, with the help of God, invest 20-25% in Small Cap Value mutual funds/ETFs to improve our risk adjusted returns over the long-term.

We will, with the help of God, evaluate our progress on our financial plan:

By tracking monthly cash flow

Checking investment performance every 6 months

Rebalancing investments once per year

Calculating Net Worth once per year

Running the Boldin Retirement Planner once per year at https://www.Boldin.com/

Check our updated Social Security benefit once per year using https://www.ssa.gov

Check our three credit reports using https://www.annualcreditreport.com once per year

We will, with the help of God, freeze our credit reports until the unlikely time we need to use credit.

We will, with the help of God, try to minimize our government taxes, while paying our fair share.

We will, with the help of God, maintain appropriate types and amounts of insurance coverage, to protect the blessings God has provided, against any unforeseen catastrophic financial events.

We will, with the help of God, sell or donate unused items to local charities such as The Salvation Army.

We will, with the help of God, be generous in our giving to help in fulfilling God's plan for our lives.

We will, with the help of God, leave a financial legacy for our child and God's mission here on earth.

LESSON 12

BEHAVIORAL FINANCE

*"Teach them His decrees and instructions,
and show them the way they are to live and how they are to behave."*
EXODUS 18:20

"Reform your ways and actions."
JEREMIAH 18:11

WHAT IS BEHAVIORAL FINANCE?

Behavioral finance is the study of what makes some individuals successful investors, while others tend to fail. It is the   we need to use to self-reflect on our personal strengths, weaknesses, and   when it comes to money and investing. Charles D. Ellis says, "The biggest risk in investing is almost always the short-term behavior of the investor. That's why '   ' is the cardinal rule for all investors. The hardest work in investing is not intellectual; it's emotional." "There are two major categories of risk in investing. One is investment risk; the other is   risk. The first gets all the attention, but the second should be our focus because, while we can do very little about investment risk, every investor can make a major difference with a moderate effort on investor risk."

THE MOST IMPORTANT THING

Howard Marks in "The Most Important Thing: Uncommon Sense for the Thoughtful Investor" writes, "The discipline that is most important (in investing) is not accounting or economics, but psychology." "The psychological factors that weigh on other investor's minds and influence their actions will weigh on yours as well…These forces tend to cause people to do the   of what a superior investor must do."

Charles D. Ellis writes, "Behavioral economists have shown that, as human beings, we are not always rational and we do not always act in our own   interests." "Self-inflicted harm applies to all investors because we ourselves cause   that are quite unnecessary and could easily be   if we would just recognize our unfortunate proclivities and discipline ourselves to do less harm, particularly to ourselves and our investments. Benign   can be good for us as investors." "Our internal demons are pride, fear, greed, exuberance, and anxiety." "The best way to start learning how to be a successful investor is to follow the standard instruction: know thyself." When it comes to understanding our financial biases the words of Paul in Romans rings true:

"I do not understand what I do. For what I want to do, I do not do, but what I hate I do." Romans 7:15

Charles D. Ellis writes, "Psychologists who study anxiety and fear have found that four characteristics make people more worried about the perceived riskiness of a situation than the realities would warrant: large-scale consequences, a lack of personal ______ or influence, unfamiliarity, and ______ occurrence."

It is no wonder people who don't expect market downturns sell on the way down or at the bottom. You must be able to continue to ______ while the market is down to achieve successful results in stock or stock mutual fund investing. Continued dollar-cost-averaging is the ______ path through a down market.

Jason Zweig says, "The secret to your financial success is inside yourself (your trust in God)...By developing your ______ and courage, you can refuse to let other people's mood swings govern your financial destiny. In the end, how your investments ______ is much less important than how ______ behave." In the words of Benjamin Graham, "Indeed, the investor's chief problem—and even his worst enemy—is likely to be himself."

There are three powerful questions we are trying to answer:

1. How can you minimize the ______ of suffering irreversible losses?
2. How can you ______ the chances of achieving sustainable gains?
3. How can you control self-defeating ______ that keeps most investors from reaching their full potential?

UNCONSCIOUS BIAS

Unconscious bias refers to biases or shortcuts our brains make, that we are unaware of and which happen outside of our control...These snap judgements don't just kick in the moment you're in danger, or need to act with an urgency, they are always present leading us to draw conclusions based on ______ or incomplete information. No matter what we actually believe or think, consciously, these little unconscious biases can cause financial harm. Once you have a handle on how your unconscious biases manifest themselves, you'll be ______ to start managing the impact your biases have on your decisions.

At their core, biases are simply mental shortcuts. They are a tool, with which we categorize the familiar and unfamiliar, the safe and the dangerous and anything else we ______ react to...A little interrogation will help you re-frame the norms you observe and reduce their effect on your unconscious bias. We're all built with blind spots. The work of being our best investing selves is to be aware of those ______ spots, and the impact they have on our investing lives. Working on your biases can be a lifetime pursuit. Examining your unconscious bias is the first step in ______ your behaviors and decisions.

We will explore some of the most commonly identified financial biases so that you, the investor, can reflect upon them and discipline yourself to recognize when you are using one or more of them in your investment decision making.

COMMON FINANCIAL BIASES

HOME BIAS

Home bias is when we favor our own employer stock shares in our 401(k), local companies, well known Blue Chip stocks or corporations whose products we use, or simply the habit of investing in what is already familiar. It is investing in the U.S. ________ market, which only represents half of investable companies world wide, while not investing in international stocks, small cap stocks or REITs.

RECENCY BIAS

Jonathan Clements writes, "Recency bias is when we assume that the current market direction will continue to be the ________ market direction, when in reality the market can reverse course at any time, or the assumption that the immediate past is ________ of the long-term future. While the long term course of the stock market has been up, expect market declines, and recognize ________ as a normal course for the stock market."

William J. Bernstein writes, "What makes recency (bias) such a killer is the fact that asset classes have a slight ________ to 'mean-revert' over periods longer than three years. Mean reversion means that periods of relatively good performance tend to be followed by periods of relatively ________ performance. The reverse also occurs; periods of relatively poor performance tend to be followed by periods of relatively ________ performance."

Howard Marks makes a very important point when he writes, "There is little I am certain of, but these things are true: ________ always prevail eventually. Nothing goes in one direction forever…And there's little that's as dangerous for investors' health (or wealth) as insistence on extrapolating ________ events into the future."

HINDSIGHT BIAS

Hindsight bias makes the market seem more ________ than it really is, causing us to pursue our current investment hunches. The winner and loser stocks or stock mutual funds are only identifiable in hindsight.

STATUS QUO BIAS

Status quo bias is the ease of making ________ changes.

OVERCONFIDENCE

Jonathan Clements writes, "Overconfidence makes us think we are more knowledgeable or ________ investors than we really are. It tends to make us more short term speculators, usually resulting in more trading in stocks and ________ stock allocations. Men tend to trade more and pursue ________ stock investment strategies than women, making women, many times, the ________ investors."

Ben Carlson writes, "Increased trading activity from overconfidence can lead to another 1.5 to 6.5 percent in relative ________." "Overconfidence is one of the biggest destroyers of wealth on the planet…It leads people to believe that they don't need to practice ________ management." "One of the most important theories to understand in the portfolio management process is Benjamin Graham's concept of margin of ________…It provides a cushion for our inability to predict the future."

William Bernstein writes, "There are really two behavioral errors operating in the overconfidence playground. The first is the 'compartmentalization' of success and failure. We tend to remember those activities, or areas of our portfolios, in which we and forget about those areas where we didn't...The second is that it's far more agreeable to ascribe success to than to luck."

The Bible speaks of overconfidence:

"They are distressed, because they had been ; they arrived there, only to be disappointed." JOB 6:20

"Do not think of yourself more than you ought, but rather think of yourself with judgement in accordance with the faith God has distributed to each of you." ROMANS 12:3

HERD BEHAVIOR

Herd behavior is following what everybody else is investing in due to widespread publicity or of the market. In the words of William J. Bernstein, "This, in turn, produces high stock prices, which result in returns. The saddest part of this story is that 'pie-in-the-sky investing' is both infectious and emotionally effortless — is doing it. Human beings are quintessentially social creatures. In most of our endeavors, this serves us well. But in the investment arena, our social are poison."

Burton Malkiel and Charles Ellis write, "Any investment that has become a topic of widespread is likely to be especially hazardous to your wealth." "Following the herd—believing 'this time is different'—has led people to make some of the investment mistakes."

"We all, like , have gone astray." ISAIAH 53:6

LOSS AVERSION

"People are far more distressed at taking than they are overjoyed at realizing gains." Researchers have found that the effect of investment losses is as powerful psychologically than investment gains.

RISK AVERSION MYOPIA

Risk aversion myopia is when "human beings experience risk in the short-term...overemphasis on the of short-term loss" instead of considering their long-term goals when making investment decisions.

RISK HORIZON

"Richard Thaler...in a...clever bit of research...estimated the risk horizon of the average investor to be year. Myopic indeed!" Some bear markets can take up to years to fully recover. Remember, you are buying stocks on sale during a bear market, and will realize the benefits of this upon the stock market recovery.

REGRET AVOIDANCE

William J Bernstein writes, "Human beings are not very good at taking losses or   failure... The most consistent bit of irrational investment behavior is the commonplace observation that we are less likely to   losers than winners. This is known in behavior finance as 'regret avoidance.' Holding onto a stock (or stock funds) that has done poorly keeps   the possibility that we will not have to confront the finality of our failure."

REPRESENTATIVENESS

William J. Bernstein writes, "Most small investors naturally   that good companies are good stocks, when the opposite is usually true. Psychologists refer to this sort of logical error as representativeness."

MENTAL ACCOUNTING

William J. Bernstein writes, "Mental accounting refers to our tendency to compartmentalize our   and unsuccessful investments, mentally separating our   and losers. This is particularly dangerous because it distracts us from what should be our main focus: the   portfolio (returns)."

ENDOWMENT EFFECT

Ben Carlson writes, "The endowment effect causes investors to   investments that they already own."

CONFIRMATION BIAS

Ben Carlson writes, "Confirmation bias draws us into only those sources that   with our current mindset instead of looking for opposing viewpoints."

AVAILABILITY BIAS

Ben Carlson writes, "An availability bias means that whatever (information) is in front of us   is what we'll base our decisions on simply because it's there."

CAPITULATION

Howard Marks describes capitulation as when "investor hold to their convictions as long as they can, but when the economic and psychological pressures (late in market up cycles) become [illegible], they surrender and jump on the bandwagon." "The tendency towards self-doubt combines with news of other people's successes to form a [illegible] force that makes investors do the wrong thing, and it gains additional strength as these trends (market going up) go on longer. It's one more influence that must be fought."

CONCLUSION

Ben Carlson writes, "Fear, greed, euphoria, panic, speculation, envy—these are the killers of your portfolio." "It doesn't matter how great an investment strategy one has if they are unable to drum up the requisite discipline to follow it over various market cycles." "Those who are able to calmly stay the course and follow their process when everyone else around them is losing their heads will be the investors that succeed at the expense of others." "Discipline is the ultimate decider between the winners and the losers in the financial markets." "The most important lessons have nothing to do with specific investments and everything to do with making good decisions and developing the correct temperament." "One of the biggest mistakes investors make is letting their emotions get in the way of making intelligent investment decisions."

Behavioral finance is the mirror we need to use to self-reflect on our strengths, weaknesses and biases when it comes to money and investing. Charles D. Ellis writes, "Four characteristics make people more worried about the perceived riskiness of a situation than the realities would warrant: large-scale consequences, a lack of personal control or influence, unfamiliarity, and sudden occurrence." While Benjamin Graham writes, "Indeed, the investor's chief problem—and even his worst enemy—is likely to be himself." The goal of this lesson is to teach the investor to control self-defeating behavior that keeps most investors from reaching their full potential.

ACTION STEPS

1. As you read through the list of behavioral biases did any of them bring back memories of investment mistakes in your past?

Focus on understanding these biases and make a plan of catching yourself before acting on your bias tendencies.

2. After reviewing the list of behavioral biases, do you believe you have set yourself up for financial success through a consistent and disciplined investment plan?

Review the rules of your investment plan to make sure they set you up for investing success during extreme market conditions.

LESSON 13

THE BEST WAY TO PURCHASE A HOME

"For every house is built by someone, but God is the builder of everything."
HEBREWS 3:4

"My people will live in peaceful dwelling places, in secure homes, in undisturbed places of rest."
ISAIAH 32:18

READINESS TO BUY A HOME

Buying a home is a complicated transaction, and becoming a homeowner is a major investment that requires __________ planning. Consumers should take a hard look at their finances to make sure they can afford to take on the financial responsibility. "A little preparation can go a long way and help you approach this __________ decision with confidence."

"It will be __________ and shade from the heat of the day, and a __________ and hiding place from the storm and rain." ISAIAH 4:6

Make sure you are __________ to buy, both emotionally and financially. Teresa Mears writes, "Look at your life, your career, your finances and your future expectations and determine whether __________ a house is the right move at this time." "Forgo buying a home until you're ready to put down roots." God desires us to settle in homes:

"Build houses and __________ down, plant gardens and eat what they produce." JEREMIAH 29:5 AND JEREMIAH 29:28

"'I will settle them in their __________,' declares the LORD." HOSEA 11:11

It is generally recommended "that buyers plan on keeping their homes for ______ years or more to increase their chances of getting a good return on their investment." This gives you the opportunity to cover your __________ costs, and makes it less likely that you would have to sell in a market downturn. "It typically takes several years for a house purchase to actually pay off. That's due to the high __________ costs of buying a home, as well as the regular expenses of homeownership."

EMERGENCY FUND

Before considering a purchase on a home you should have three to nine months of __________ savings set aside in an online high yield savings account or money market mutual fund. This emergency savings fund should be above and __________ your planned down payment on a home and your closing costs.

REVIEW YOUR CREDIT FIRST

Go to annualcreditreport.com and get a free credit report from each of the major credit services: TransUnion, Equifax, and Experian. Examine your credit reports for any errors. Gina Pogol writes, "Many credit reports contain erroneous data...which can lower your credit score and cost you of dollars, or even keep you from getting a loan." "With less than 20 percent down, the lower credit score (below 680) you will also see higher costs for Private Mortgage Insurance (PMI)...."

The Motley Fool recommends, "To get the most competitive (mortgage) interest rate—and the most loan—you'll need a good credit score." "One in people have errors on their credit report, and these errors could result in your score being lower than it should."

Also find out your FICO score, a three digit number between 300 to 850. FICO defines the "good" range as 670 to 739. This is what most lenders use to determine the terms of your mortgage (how much interest rate they plan to charge you). Maryalene LaPonsie writes, "Spend time to get your credit in the best possible shape so that you can get the most terms from lenders." Don't give out your social security number to every lender to review your FICO score, simply ask the first lender what your score is, and pass that information on to other lenders. "Lenders save their interest rates for homebuyers with the best credit scores."

Deborah Kearns writes, "If your credit score is below 620, you will have trouble getting approved for a mortgage. To qualify for an FHA loan, you'll need a minimum credit score of 580 to use the program's maximum financing of 3.5% down payment, or a minimum score of 500 with a 10% down payment."

"If you have obvious issues—a history of late payments, debt collection actions, or significant debt—it could mean less-than-ideal rates and terms, or even outright denial. It can take at least year to improve a low credit score. Boost your score by paying on time, making more than the minimum monthly payments on debts, and not out your available credit."

"Some states offer grants to help with a down payment or closing costs, especially for time home buyers in certain public service professions. You may also qualify for FHA or VA loans that... impose requirements on consumers trying to get into a home for the first time."

SAVE FOR YOUR DOWN PAYMENT AND CLOSING COSTS

"Suppose one of you wants to build a tower (home). Won't you first sit down and estimate the cost to see if you have enough money to complete it? For if you lay the foundation and are not able to finish it, everyone who sees it will ridicule you, saying, 'This person began to build and wasn't able to finish.'" Luke 14:28-30

Ideally it would be best to try to save for a 20% down payment, or better yet, buy your home for cash. But that is just not possible for most of us. Maryalene LaPonsie writes, "As the Consumer Financial Protection Bureau says: 'In general, the money you put down upfront the money you will pay in interest and fees over the life of the loan. And if you put down less than 20%, be prepared for Private Mortgage Insurance (PMI) premium as part of your escrow.

"You can use a gift from a relative or friend toward your ______ payment. However, many loan products require a gift ______ and documentation to source the deposit and verify that the donor isn't expecting you to pay ______ the money."

The Motley Fool writes, "You need a down payment, which can range from as little as nothing (for USDA or VA loans), 3.5% to 10% for a FHA loan, to 10% or 20% for conventional financing. But that's not all. You'll still have to pay loan closing costs which could total about 2% to 5% of the home's ______ price. There are also other items, such as ______ accounts for homeowners insurance, property taxes, and PMI if necessary." "Private Mortgage Insurance (PMI) typically costs between 0.5% and 1.0% of the entire ______ amount."

"Homebuyers in the U.S. pay, on average, $5,749 for closing cost, according to a 2019 survey from ClosingCorp, a real estate closing cost data firm." Understand ______ costs before you close on a home. "There are required expenses, including loan origination fee; home appraisal costs; the costs of a home survey; title insurance premiums; prorated property taxes; transfer taxes; and more."

"It can take some potential homeowners ______ years to save for the down payment and closing costs, above and beyond their 3-9 month emergency fund. Adding closing costs to your mortgage loan is a ______ bad idea. "Not only will you end up paying interest on closing costs over decades, but it could trigger PMI if you're borrowing more than 20% of a home's value."

YOU NEED CASH RESERVES

Gina Pogol points out you also need cash reserves. "Then there are also reserve requirements—many lenders require borrowers to have enough in the ______ to pay their mortgage for at least ______ months if they have an interruption in income." If you have a fully funded ______ fund you have that covered. Furthermore, you may need to make deposits to utilities and cable companies and the like to start services.

Teresa Mears writes, "Don't spend all your ______. It costs money to move, change locks, put down utility deposits, and buy things like a lawnmower." "If you don't have cash for a down payment, closing costs" and an emergency fund, you may be better off ______ to purchase a home.

ORGANIZE AND UPDATE YOUR DOCUMENTS

Mortgage lenders are going to want to get a ______ picture of your financial wellbeing before offering you terms on a loan. Keep all your documents: bank statements, W-2s, deposit records, tax returns, pay stubs, retirement and brokerage account statements organized and ______ so you can provide documentation when your lender requests it.

"When you apply for your mortgage, the loan application will be reviewed with a fine-toothed comb. Anything you claim on the application will be ______ and must be documented, including your income, any assets you are using for a down payment, closing costs and those for reserves. If the source of your down payment is a gift from family or others, you'll need a gift letter from the ______ (preferably notarized)."

God's Word tells us that we are to get our income ready prior to buying or building a home:

"Put your outdoor work in order and get your fields ______; after that, build your house."
PROVERBS 24:27

HOMEOWNERS INSURANCE

Homeowners insurance is something the mortgage company will let you go without. The cost of homeowners insurance will be and become part of your monthly mortgage payment.

"A flood will off his house, rushing waters on the day of God's wrath. Such is the fate God allots to the wicked, the heritage appointed for them by God" JOB 20:28-29

"The LORD tears the house of the proud." PROVERBS 15:2 / PROVERBS 15:25

APPLY FOR A MORTGAGE WITH A FEW LENDERS

You should "apply for a mortgage with a few lenders to get a better sense of what you can afford and clearer of loan products, interest rates, closing costs, and lender fees." "You will need to actually lenders and get Loan Estimate Disclosures (formerly called the 'Good Faith Estimate of Closing Costs'), which are actual interest rate and fee commitments from that they must honor."

"The Consumer Financial Protection Bureau says nearly of mortgage borrowers don't shop around...and fail to look for a better mortgage rate." "Shopping for a mortgage puts you in a better position to with lenders to get the best deal possible." "As you shop lenders, pay attention to fees and closing costs." "There are a few fees that have the most room for negotiation including: Loan Origination Fee, Application Fee, Broker Fee, and Underwriting Fee." "Keep in mind that some lenders will offer you discount 'points,' a way to down your interest rate upfront." You'll pay for these 'points' at closing to secure the interest rate.

SHOPPING YOUR MORTGAGE

"When you buy a mortgage you'll have the option of paying 'points.' A typically costs 1% of your total mortgage amount and lowers your interest rate by around a quarter of a percent (0.25%). To determine if you should pay points, see how long it will take to break from the up-front costs." "Understanding points is essential to decide whether to them, and to make certain that you are comparing apples-to-apples when shopping for a loan."

The Motley Fool writes, "The reality is, there can be differences in terms from one lender to another. And, when you're taking on such a large debt, even differences in the interest rate affect your finances in big ways. To get the most affordable mortgage, apply with lenders." "Compare offers and pay attention to details, such as whether you have to pay points to get a lower interest rate...look for a loan that has the lowest costs, including closing costs and interest over time."

MORTGAGE LOANS TO AVOID

"Mortgage loans with a balloon payment and - mortgages are two good examples of high-risk loans, but there are others...including adjustable rate mortgages (ARMs) you couldn't if rates go up." "ARMs have lower initial rates than fixed-rate mortgages. Interest rates on these mortgages periodically. When that happens, your rate could rise, making your (monthly) payments larger." "If you don't understand the terms, don't sign for the loan."

Maryalene LaPonsie writes, "Avoid interest only loans and be careful about using an adjustable-rate mortgage (ARM) especially in an environment. They begin with low payments, but the interest rate adjusts (higher) later on and can take your skywards." "A fixed-rate mortgage, on the other hand, gives stability, security and of mind."

IF BUDGET ALLOWS—SHORTEN YOUR TERM

If you can afford a 15 or 20 year fixed rate mortgage instead of a 30 year fixed rate mortgage, without strapping your monthly flow, by all means do it. You'll be mortgage that much faster. If you think a 30 year fixed rate is better for your overall budget, you can always add an extra amount with each payment to accelerate prepayment of the mortgage loan.

GET A MORTGAGE PRE-APPROVAL LETTER PRIOR TO SHOPPING

"Get pre-approved for a mortgage—a process where you actually start a mortgage application with a lender and receive a commitment for a mortgage...This is vital in active and housing markets." "Sellers are more likely to consider offers from buyers who have a pre-approval from a lender." "A seller feels more confident selecting a bid from someone with a mortgage pre-approval." "The pre-approval letter also includes an expiration , usually within 90 days."

HOW MUCH SHOULD I SPEND ON A HOME?

As a general rule, it is best to limit your housing costs to 25-30% or less of your home pay. That 25-30 percent figure should encompass not just your actual mortgage payment, but also your escrowed property taxes, homeowners insurance, and Private Mortgage Insurance (PMI) if you're not putting at least 20% down on the mortgage. Oftentimes, the property taxes, homeowners insurance and PMI are escrowed by the mortgage servicer into an account and become part of the PITI (Principle, Interest, Taxes, Insurance) or one lump monthly payment. To play it even safer, you might even decide that the 25-30% limit should include ongoing maintenance costs.

"When a lender tells you that you can borrow up to $300,000, it doesn't mean you should. Typically, most prospective homeowners can afford a loan amount between 2 and 2.5 times their annual income." "Buying a more expensive house than you can reasonably afford can land you in if you have to stretch your monthly budget to make mortgage payments. In other words, you might end up feeling 'house poor' and experience remorse...and stretching your monthly budget...will eat up your cash flow for other goals." "The bank sets the maximum limit based on the limited financial information available—but doesn't understand the of your financial life."

"Borrowing up to the bank approval limit may your finances and set you up for catastrophe in the event of a loss (or uninsured disability). Consider shaving at least off the bank approved amount and use that as your maximum price when house hunting."

"A mortgage qualification can show you how a comfortable payment translates to a home purchase price. Meera Jagannathan writes, "Figure out how much house you can afford. Use a home affordability calculator to get a estimate, and then be even more conservative. Make sure you're focusing on what the monthly looks like for that mortgage, versus the overall loan amount." "Then, you can your search to affordable properties that won't break the budget."

Maurie Backman writes, "Why shouldn't you spend more on housing? It's simple: If you exceed that 30% threshold, you might to cover your remaining bills, not to mention your homeownership costs themselves. And that puts you at risk for racking up dangerous card debt, or even potentially losing your home to foreclosure if it becomes too difficult to afford."

By keeping housing costs on the lower side, and buying a home well below the of your price range, it gives you leeway for other financial goals. It will allow you to steadily fund your retirement accounts, pay for childcare, fund a college 529 plan, and a host of other things that would have not been possible if you bought a more home. Buying a less expensive home gives you the option to spend more money on things that bring you like traveling, giving your kids the opportunity of enriching after school activities, and dining out. If you would rather spend your money experiencing life the walls of your home, keeping housing expenses low should be a priority when house hunting.

Stacy Johnson re-iterates the importance of not buying too much house when he writes, If "you let vanity replace sense, you buy more house than you need, leave no margin for error, and end up furnishing, heating, cooling, maintaining and paying taxes on you don't use." "Determine what you (as opposed to want) and spend as little as possible to get it. There's no reason to create unnecessary by over-leveraging."

HOME MAINTENANCE COSTS

"Estimate around 1% of the of the home will be spent on repairs each year." "The expense many new homeowners are not prepared (for)...is maintenance, which averaged about $ in 2020, according to home improvement marketplace HomeAdvisor." Neglecting maintenance comes with consequences!

"Through laziness, the rafters ; because of idle hands, the house leaks." ECCLESIASTES 10:18

LOCATION, LOCATION, LOCATION: DETERMINE WHERE YOU WANT TO BUY

Dima Williams recommends, "Home shoppers moving to new areas should consider for a while, even if they have the means to buy a house. This strategy allows 'would-be' homeowners to 'test-drive' a neighborhood, its schools and amenities." "Renting gives you the to make the right decision...The single biggest decision anyone has to make is, 'Where do I want my family to live?' If you don't know, renting takes a little bit of the pressure off."

"Live in it, trade in it, and property in it." GENESIS 34:10

"And I will a place for my people…and will plant them so that they can have a home." 2 SAMUEL 7:10 / 1 CHRONICLES 17:9

"I (God) have been with you you have gone." 1 CHRONICLES 17:8

Teresa Mears writes, "Choose your location first." "Decide where you want to live. Talk to friends, coworkers and neighbors in the prospective neighborhood. Go to houses." God promises to help us with making this decision:

"He determines the times set for them and the places where they should live." ACTS 17:26

"The land on which your feet have will be your inheritance and that of your children forever, because you have the LORD my God wholeheartedly." JOSHUA 14:9

CONSIDER RESALE VALUE

Consider resale value you purchase a home. "There are certain features that make houses more or less likely to to buyers. Location is a big one, as few people want to buy the home in the neighborhood. School districts, the general property market in your area, and a home's condition can also impact value." It is better to buy a lower priced home in a home neighborhood, as this will lift your future home's value.

"A spacious land that has put into your hands, a land that nothing whatever." JUDGES 18:10

"The land is still ours, because we the LORD our God…So they and prospered." 2 CHRONICLES 14:7

"They acquired there and were fruitful." GENESIS 47:27

DETERMINE YOUR LOCATION AND PRICE AND USE THE INTERNET

"Look for homes on the internet, evaluating style, size, price, and how they stay on the market."

- Best Overall Website: Zillow at https://www.zillow.com
- Most Accurate Website: Realtor.com Multiple Listing Service (MLS)
- Best Mobile App: Trulia
- Best for Foreclosures: Foreclosure.com
- Best "For Sale By Owner": FSBO.com

According to the 2020 National Association of REALTORS Profile of Home Buyers and Sellers,

- 51% of buyers found the home they purchased on the internet
- 28% found the home they bought through their realtor
- 7% found the home they bought through a yard sign

FINDING A BUYER'S REALTOR AGENT

"For most people,it's a mistake to go it through the homebuying process." "If you're a , there is no reason not to use a real estate agent (as their fee is paid by the seller and split between the seller and buyer's agent)." "You want people who have worked and have experience directly in the you're looking in." "After you've found the house, you'll most need the agent, both to structure and present the and then troubleshoot issues that arise between contract and closing." "A good agent can direct you to properties entering the market…and generally smooth out the bumps that may arise."

Miranda Marquit writes, "A good buyer's agent is required to help you, the buyer." "Look for a buyer's agent solely focused on finding you the home…Also pay attention to whether the agent to you and makes you feel comfortable. If you get an agent that isn't a fit, don't be afraid to walk away."

WHAT TO LOOK FOR WHEN EVALUATING HOMES

Teresa Mears writes, "Know what's important to you. If you're on a first-time buyers budget, you have to be about what you can afford. No house will be perfect, so where are you to compromise?" "You might have to choose between a smaller house in a specific school district or close to work, or a larger house with a longer commute in a new neighborhood. If you find of what you're looking for, you're doing pretty good."

"When you look at houses, focus on the right things. Focus on the things you change. For example, you can't easily add another bedroom, a better location or a more functional floor plan. Even for easy updates, evaluate how much the work will cost and if you have the to do the work yourself, and whether after closing you'll have the to make the changes right away." "Be ready to move (on a contract) once you find the home you want. Good homes that are well priced nearly always quickly." Make sure you buy based on reality and not emotion. "Some people see a house they love and their planned goes out the window."

WRITING A PURCHASE AGREEMENT

"The purchase/sale agreement you enter into sets the for much more than just the total you'll pay. The contract should contain to protect you (in case) the house fails a home or you can't get financing (or can't sell your current home)." "Consider what contingencies you want in the contract or you're willing to waive. A purchase offer is usually contingent on a satisfactory inspection, approval of your mortgage and an appraisal that is equal to or than the purchase price." The Bible instructs us to offer a fair price:

"If you sell land to any of your own people or buy land from them, do not take of each other." LEVITICUS 25:14

INSIST ON A HOME INSPECTION

"Regardless of whether you're buying new construction or a historic home, you need to have it ______ before finalizing the sale. Don't trust your own judgement. A professional will be able to point out possible ______ violations, safety threats and structural damage." Dori Zinn writes, "During a home inspection, a professionally trained inspector visually and physically evaluates the entire ______ from the foundation all the way up to the roof, looking for potential defects or red flags." "To make the most of the inspection, try to ______ through the house with the inspector so he or she can point out potential problems and you can ______ questions." Many inspectors share pointers for taking care of your new home, and provide written information regarding caring for your home.

We need to thoroughly inspect the property prior to purchase.

"Go and make a ______ of the land and write a description of it." JOSHUA 18:8

"Go, walk ______ the length and breadth of the land, for I (______) am giving it to you." GENESIS 13:17

We need to get a professional home inspection to determine the soundness of the home. Of special concern is the foundation. Jesus says,

"As for everyone who comes to me and hears My words and puts them into practice…They are like a man building a house, who dug down ______ and laid the foundation on rock. When a flood came, the torrent struck the house but could not shake it, because it was ______ built." LUKE 6:47-48

"The house of the righteous ______ firm." PROVERBS 12:7

"Look carefully for a good independent ______ with a great reputation for helping home buyers ensure a house is structurally sound and ______ of major defects." "You can find a qualified house inspector through the American Society of Home Inspectors (ASHI), or get a recommendation from your real estate agent or community members."

"Include a home inspection contingency that gives you a penalty-free ______ from the deal if a major issue is uncovered and the seller is unwilling to fix it before closing. With that contingency in place you can ______ your offer and usually get your ______ earnest money deposit refunded." "The home inspection fee is non-refundable and typically paid by the ______ to the home inspector upfront. It typically ranges from $300 to $500, depending on location and the size of the property."

KEEP FINANCES STABLE BETWEEN CONTRACT AND CLOSING

"Keep your credit and ______ stable until you close on your new home." "You might want to wait a few months before adding more monthly payments for big purchases to the mix." You should also keep your ______ stable. "While changing jobs may benefit your career, it may complicate your mortgage approval." "If you start ______ up a storm before closing, you're throwing off your debt-to-income ratio and are at risk of the bank deciding ______ to lend to you."

COMPARE CLOSING DOCUMENT WITH LOAN ESTIMATE DISCLOSURE

Lenders are _____ to provide you with a five-page Closing Disclosure three days prior to closing. Take the time to compare it against the initial loan estimate _____ you received to make sure you aren't being charged extra fees by your lender or other parties involved in the transaction. Come to closing prepared to _____ a host of paperwork and with a certified check or cashier's check to cover all the closing costs.

"Finally, don't sign anything you don't _____ or feel comfortable with. Ask questions and expect answers—and if you don't understand them, ask for better explanations."

CLOSING DOCUMENTS

"I signed and sealed the _____, had it witnessed, and weighed out the _____ on the scales. I took the deed of purchase—the sealed copy containing the _____ and conditions, as well as the unsealed copy...This is what the LORD Almighty...says: 'Take these documents, both the sealed and unsealed copies of the deed of purchase, and put them in a clay jar (_____) so they will last a long time...Fields will be bought for silver and deeds will be signed, sealed and witnessed...because I will restore their _____,' declares the LORD." JEREMIAH 32:10-11, 14, AND 44

PRIVATE MORTGAGE INSURANCE (PMI)

If your loan includes PMI, keep track of your _____ as you continue to make mortgage payments, and the housing market continues to rise. Once you can establish 20% equity in your home, you can ask your mortgage _____ to remove the PMI from your escrow and payment. This will _____ valuable dollars as you continue to pay down your mortgage.

PROPERTY TAXES WILL PROBABLY RISE AFTER CLOSING

"Homebuyers need to understand that property taxes likely will be _____ based on their purchase transaction—which means _____ could potentially rise."

HOUSING MARKET UNCERTAINTY

"Even experts struggle to _____ trends in the real estate market." Like the stock market, don't try to _____ the housing market. Just be careful if you're in a housing market that turns into _____ wars, and you are too eager to make a purchase. That's when the budget and important contingencies get thrown out the window, and you could make a _____ you'll regret later. Instead "you can research metrics...such as average days on the market before a sale." The fewer those days, the more _____ the real estate market.

VIEWING YOUR HOME AS AN INVESTMENT

Steven Keys gives us a proper ________ on viewing our homes as ________ protection when he writes, "Houses are often sold as wealth-building tools—a way to escape 'throwing money away' on rent." "It's important to realize that (housing price appreciation)...represents an annualized appreciation of 3.5%. That's right in line with ________ over the same period. There will be booms and busts, but in inflation-adjusted terms, the average real ________ of single-family homes is pretty close to zero over long periods of time." "While your home's value probably won't outpace inflation, it's saving you money in the form of foregone ________ payments along the way."

IS BUYING A BIGGER HOME A BETTER INVESTMENT?

"Traditional thinking leads people to believe that buying bigger and bigger homes is no problem at all, because the returns on that investment ________ with the price paid…this simply isn't true. Price appreciation is gobbled up by inflation, so the only thing left in your return-on-investment calculation is ________ rent payments. The amount in rent doesn't increase when you buy a bigger house, so by spending more, you're ________ your return."

"The children…will yet say in your hearing, 'This place is too ________ for us; give us more space to live in.'" ISAIAH 49:20

Steven Keys puts things in a proper perspective when he writes, "The logical conclusion is that buying a ________ expensive house costs you less money (and makes you ________) over time. It almost sounds like common sense, but it's a fundamental point that is ________ on too many people." "The house you live in can certainly be a wealth-building tool, but it is important to have realistic expectations about how it might ________ as an investment."

Dima Williams points out, "Over the long run, ________ investing is often more profitable than buying a residence, especially after accounting for homeownership ________ … home value appreciation tends to be ________ than what the stock market returns."

CONCLUSION

You shouldn't purchase a home unless you intend to stay in it for at least five years. Before you begin looking for a home, get your finances in order. This includes a fully funded emergency fund, ideally a 20% down payment, and closing costs. Make sure your credit report is up to snuff so that you will receive the best terms on your new mortgage. Organize and update your documents prior to meeting with mortgage lenders. Shop with a few different lenders in order to get the best rate and terms on your mortgage. Get a mortgage pre-approval letter from your lender prior to shopping for a home. The general rule is to limit your housing costs to 25-30% or less of your take home pay. View your home as an inflationary hedge. Do not use your home as an asset in your retirement calculations, unless you intend to sell and downsize, using the difference to invest for retirement.

ACTION STEPS

1. If you are considering the purchase of a new home, do you have your finances in order including a fully funded emergency fund, a 20% down payment, and closing costs?
2. Do you have a secure job, and intend to stay in the home your are looking to buy for at least 5 years?
3. Have you checked your credit reports, and maximized your credit score?
4. Have you collected all the paperwork the mortgage provider needs to write you a pre-approval letter? Have you shopped different mortgage providers for the best rate?
5. Do you have a pre-approval letter from your chosen mortgage lender? Have you locked in your interest rate?
6. Have you chosen a community in which you would like to live? If you're planning on having children, what is the reputation of the school district?
7. Have you searched the internet for homes in this area, and do they fall in your price range? Can you find plenty of housing options in this community within your price range?
8. Have you found a buyer's real estate agent to help you with your search, and to write the contract with appropriate contingencies?

LESSON 14

PREPARING FOR AND LIVING IN RETIREMENT

"I thought, 'Age should speak; advanced years should teach wisdom.' But it is the spirit in a person, the breath of the Almighty, that gives them understanding. It is not only the aged who understand what is right. 'Therefore I say: Listen to me; I too will tell you what I know.'"

JOB 32:7-10

"I was young and now I am old, yet I have never seen the righteous forsaken or their children begging bread."

PSALM 37:25

BEFORE YOU RETIRE DETERMINE YOUR PURPOSE

Study after study shows that defining your purpose in life is key to retirement happiness.

"Grey hair is a crown of splendor; it is attained in the way of ______________." PROVERBS 16:31

"Is not wisdom found among the aged? Does not long ______________ bring understanding?" JOB 12:12

Brandon Ballenger writes: "The following are the most popular sources of purpose, meaning and fulfillment, according to a 2021 report from Edward Jones:"

1. Spending Time with Loved Ones: A whopping 67% of retirees and 61% of pre-retirees name spending time with loved ones as a source of purpose and meaning in retirement. "Enjoy life with your ______________, whom you love, all the days of this…life that God has given you under the sun." Ecclesiastes 9:9 or the words of Psalm 71:18, "Even when I am old and gray, do not forsake me, my God, till I declare your power to the ______________ generation, your mighty acts to all who are to come."
2. Doing Interesting and Enjoyable Things: Fifty-five percent of retirees and 64% of pre-retirees expect to find meaning and fulfillment in doing interesting and enjoyable things. Ecclesiastes 11:8 says,"However many years anyone may live, let them ______________ them all."
3. Being True to Myself: Fifty-three percent of retirees and 43% of pre-retirees named "being true to myself" as a source of purpose, meaning, and fulfillment. Retirement can be a surprising time of self-discovery or reinvention. Consider the words of Paul in Romans 12:2, "Do not conform any longer to the pattern of this world, but be ______________ by the renewing of your mind. Then you will be able to test and approve what God's will is—His good, pleasing and ______________ will."
4. Being Generous and Giving Back: Forty percent of retirees and 31% of pre-retirees ranked highly, being generous, as a source of purpose and fulfillment. In 2 Corinthians 9:8 it says, "And God is able to bless you ______________, so that in all things at all times, having all that you need, you will abound in every good work."

5. Living a Faith-filled Life: Thirty-eight percent of retirees and 34% of pre-retirees cited living a faith-filled life as a source of purpose in retirement. Retirees also cite faith and values among the most important contributors to their identity in retirement. In the words of Acts 20:24, "My only aim is to finish the race and complete the the Lord Jesus has given me—the task of to the good news of God's grace."
6. Living a Joyful Life: Thirty-two percent of retirees and 41% of pre-retirees intend to find meaning by living a joyful life. Once you've done a lifetime of work to get to retirement it's time to spend on activities that bring joy to your life. 1 Thessalonians 5:16 tells us to, "Be joyful ; pray continually; give thanks in all circumstances, for this is God's will for you in Christ Jesus."
7. Fulfilling My Life Goals: Twenty-one percent of retirees and 31% of pre-retirees say, "fulfilling my life goals," will provide meaning in retirement. Consider the goal of Paul in Philippians 3:14, "I press on toward the to win the prize for which God has called me heavenward in Christ Jesus."
8. Being Financially Wealthy: Sixteen percent of retirees and 27% of pre-retirees say wealth is one of the greatest sources of fulfillment in retirement. Jesus warns against the pride of the rich in The Parable of the Rich Fool: "You have plenty of grain laid up for many years. 'Take life easy; eat, drink, and be merry.'...This night your will be demanded of you...This is how it will be with whoever stores up things for themselves but is not toward God." LUKE 12:16-21

ARE YOU FOLLOWING GOD'S PLAN FOR FINANCIAL (IN)DEPENDENCE?

If you have been following through with your personal financial plan as outlined in Lesson 11 "Having A Financial Plan," then your retirement plan is just an of this overall financial plan, and you are well on your way to a retirement. If you have neglected the earlier advice, TODAY is the day to get yourself and family back on track.

Questions you should consider are: Do you have a fully funded emergency fund? Are you living debt free? Is your mortgage paid off? Are you your faith community? Are you investing of your salary in tax advantaged savings vehicles, or using catch-up contributions to get you back on track? Do you have appropriate coverage to protect your family from possible disaster? If you can answer YES to all these questions you are well on your way to a secure retirement.

KNOWING YOUR RETIREMENT FINANCIAL NUMBERS

Figuring out if you can retire financially secure can be a complicated and perplexing question to answer. Consider these words from the Bible:

"Now listen, you who say, 'Today or tomorrow we will go to this or that city, spend a year there, carry on business and make .' Why, you do not even know what will happen tomorrow. What is your life? You are a mist that appears for a and then vanishes. Instead, you ought to say, 'If it is the Lord's , we will live and do this or that.'" JAMES 4:13-15

Finding the answers to each of the following Retirement Numbers will give you the information you need to make an informed decision on your financial readiness to retire. Kathleen Coxwell in her online article, "16 Retirement Numbers You Need to Know for a Secure Future," writes:

RETIREMENT NUMBER 1: YOUR FINANCIAL INDEPENDENCE NUMBER (FI)?

This FI Number is achieved when you have enough ____________ savings or passive income to cover all your expenses for as long as you will be alive. Most FI proponents suggest that you can achieve FI when you have amassed enough investment savings to cover ______ times one year's worth of expenses.

"Let perseverance finish its work so that you may be mature and complete, not ________ anything." JAMES 1:4

RETIREMENT NUMBER 2: FINANCIAL INDEPENDENCE RATIO?

Your FI RATIO will tell you how close you are to achieving FI. Divide your ______ ________ by your FI number. The resulting percentage will mark your progress toward FI, and is a good way to ____________ your readiness for retirement.

RETIREMENT NUMBER 3: YOUR SOCIAL SECURITY START AGE?

You probably know that the later you start Social Security, the higher your monthly benefit will be. Did you know that the lump sum value of all your Social Security benefits is likely to be ____________ than the total of all your retirement savings? You should use a Social Security optimizer program to determine the ________ age for you and your spouse to claim benefits.

RETIREMENT NUMBER 4: HOW LONG WILL YOU LIVE?

Use a good longevity calculator to best determine you and your spouses ____________ length of life. We must invest for a long life:

"I will give you a ______ lifespan." EXODUS 23:26

"Even to your old age and gray hairs I am He. I am He who will ____________ you, I have made you and I will carry you, I will sustain you…." ISAIAH 46:4

RETIREMENT #5: HOW MUCH MONTHLY GUARANTEED LIFETIME INCOME DO YOU HAVE?

This number is the real financial __________ of lifetime financial security. Retirees who report having guaranteed income that exceeds their spending report less ________ and an overall more __________ retirement. Common sources of guaranteed lifetime income include: Social Security, pensions and ____________ annuities—add them up to get this important retirement number. Many retirees who have adequate savings buy a lifetime __________ to insure their retirement income.

"God has been gracious to me, and I have ______ I need." GENESIS 33:11

RETIREMENT NUMBER 6: INFLATION OUTLOOK (%)

Inflation in retirement—when you are living off a fixed set of assets, inflation means you buy with your money every year. You typically want to invest your nest egg just enough so that the money in your is earning more than the rate of inflation.

RETIREMENT NUMBER 7: RATE OF RETURN OF INVESTMENT PORTFOLIO?

The rate of investment returns varies greatly depending on the of the time period you are looking at, and the type of investments and the allocation your portfolio is holding. Remember there is always increased with increased reward, and in the five years prior to retiring and the five years after retiring your portfolio risk should be the conservative.

RETIREMENT NUMBER 8: OUT OF POCKET HEALTHCARE COSTS?

Fidelity's 21st annual Retiree Health Care Cost Estimate has done us all a big favor by estimating the average out of pocket cost for a 65 year old couple retiring in 2022, over the course of their remaining projected lifetimes=$315,000(women $165,000, men $150,000). For some this may not be a shock, but to most of the and unprepared, this number may represent a total expense greater than their current portfolio.

RETIREMENT NUMBER 9: ESTIMATED MONTHLY RETIREMENT SPENDING?

Knowing how much you spend each month is another critically important number. If you have been this number should be easy to identify. The importance of course is that the more you spend the more investment savings and income you'll need. Most experts recommend using of what you spent while working, although in the early years if you plan to travel this number may be greater than 100%.

RETIREMENT NUMBER 10: HOW MUCH IS YOUR HOME WORTH?

This number is important since many people going into retirement have more home than they have in retirement savings. Downsizing, or selling your home and renting, while investing the remaining home equity may be way to bolster your retirement income.

RETIREMENT NUMBER 11: HOW MUCH HAVE YOU SAVED IN RETIREMENT ACCOUNTS?

This number is simple enough to find. Just add up all your different accounts taken from your most recent statements, or acquire an accounting to today's date.

RETIREMENT NUMBER 12: YOUR RETIREMENT AGE

Define your retirement age as, when you stop earning from work, or maybe the age when you need to rely on from investment savings to make ends meet.

RETIREMENT NUMBER 13: THE INVESTMENT SAVINGS YOU NEED FOR RETIREMENT?

This is THE retirement number—the one question everyone wants answered. The best way to get a reliable answer is to use a good retirement calculator that can be completely personalized. My personal favorite choice is the Boldin Retirement Planner, but I'm sure any of the large brokerage firms, ________ simulations, will give you a quality answer. A Monte Carlo analysis uses a computer to do thousands of calculations to predict a wide range of outcomes including a worst case scenario, a ________ case scenario, and a best case scenario.

RETIREMENT NUMBER 14: YOUR NET WORTH?

This is a simple calculation that you should be tracking ________ your financial life. It is simply: Net Worth=The Value of all your Assets minus all your Debts. Net Worth is considered the most ________ measure of wealth.

RETIREMENT NUMBER 15: PROJECTED ESTATE VALUE?

The projected value of your estate is the ________ Net Worth at your projected life expectancy.

"I will give them ________ of heart and action, so that they will always fear Me and that all will go ________ for them and their children after them." JEREMIAH 32:39

RETIREMENT NUMBER 16: THE VALUE OF YOUR EMERGENCY FUND?

This should be an easy number to come by for those who have been ________ a consistent God honoring financial plan.

SOCIAL SECURITY

Social security is meant to replace only ________ of pre-retirement income. It is important to know your Full Retirement Age (FRA). "This is important to know because after your FRA your Social Security benefit increases for every month you do not claim up to age 70, at about ________ per year, while your benefit is decreased by ~8% per year for every month you claim prior to your FRA with the earliest allowable claim at age 62 years."

"Social Security uses your 35 highest earning years to calculate your benefit. Working longer allows those lower earning years to be ________ by higher earning years in their calculation, another benefit to a delayed claim until age 70 years. The amount of your benefit is based on a formula that is meant to be actuarially ________. That basically means you should get the same total amount of benefits over the course of your retirement regardless of the age at which you claim benefits, ________ you live longer than your actuarial death (women 87/men 84) at which time a higher benefit will result in increased benefits over your lifetime. Also a higher initial Social Security benefit will be compounded over time at a greater ________ than a smaller Social Security benefit when taking into account the (COLA) Cost of Living Adjustments given as a percentage increase in benefit."

OPTIMAL CLAIMING OF SOCIAL SECURITY

Chris Kissel writes, "About 21% of workers at risk of being unable to afford retirement would improve their situation if they started Social Security benefits at the _____ time. Poverty among the elderly could be cut by nearly _____ if all retirees claimed Social Security at the financially optimal time."

"There are a number of companies specializing in a custom analysis of Social Security claiming strategies including:

Kiplinger	$49.95
Social Security Choices	$39.99
Social Security Choices (with coupon code "moneytalks")	$29.99

USING A LIFE EXPECTANCY CALCULATOR

Kathleen Coxwell writes, "If you're going to stress test your retirement assumptions you need to have a realistic idea of how _____ you may live, to test the sustainability of your plan for you and your spouse's _____ lifetime. The best way to do this is to use a Life Expectancy Calculator that will ask you a number of health related questions and spit out your life expectancy.

"Show me, LORD, my life's _____ and the number of my days; let me know how fleeting my life is."
PSALM 39:4

Although these life expectancy calculators won't show you God's _____ time for your death, they will give you a sense of what you should plan for in your retirement plan. Some Life Expectancy Calculators you could use:

Livingto100	Blue Zones Vitality Compass
Blueprint Income	LifeSpan (Northwestern Mutual)
John Hancock Life Expectancy Calculator	Big Life

LIFE EXPECTANCY

Here are a few additional facts from the Society of Actuaries and the Social Security Administration:

- One-third of males and one-half of females in their mid-fifties will live to be 90.
- For a couple who is 65, there is a 50% chance that one person will be alive at 92.
- If you live to be 65, you will likely live another 20 years, on average.
- If you live to be 75, the average life expectancy is 88.
- If you live to be 85, the average life expectancy is 92.
- If you live to be 95, the average life expectancy is 98.

"In His hand is the _____ of every creature and the breath of all mankind." JOB 12:10

"As no one has power over the wind to contain it, so no one has _____ over the time of their death."
ECCLESIASTES 8:8

ARE YOU FINANCIALLY PREPARED?

"One person dies in full vigor, completely and at ease, well nourished in body, bone rich with marrow. Another dies in bitterness of soul, never having enjoyed good. Side by side they lie in the dust, and worms cover them both." JOB 21:23-26

"For many in the United States who have yet to take seriously saving for retirement, living in poverty will be the end result. According to a recent GOBankingRates study ~42% of Americans have less than $10,000 for retirement." "Not enough people are actively saving for retirement. One in four ( ) of workers surveyed have no savings at all. The Insured Retirement Institute survey found that 51% of the polled have less than $50,000 saved."

"If only they were wise and would understand this and what their end will be!" DEUTERONOMY 32:29

THERE IS NO TIME LIKE THE PRESENT TO SAVE

The sooner you start the less you'll have to save, because of the miracle of interest, to reach your goals. If you have at least 15 years before your retirement, you still have a good chance of saving $500,000, a decent nest egg. According to IRI 20% of American workers have more than $500,000 saved, and only 8% have at least $1 million saved.

"They spend their years in and go down to the grave in peace." JOB 21:13

Chris Kissel writes, "According to a federal government calculator this is how much you have to save per year to reach your goal of $500,000 over 15 years based on various rates of return for your investment portfolio:

Annual Rate of Return	Annual Amount Saved	Total Amount Saved
5%	$23,500	$507,009.93
8%	$18,000	$502,096.89
10%	$16,000	$508,232.62
12%	$13,500	$503,276.15

You cannot control the market's annual rate of return, but you can control how much you spend and . It is probably more realistic to expect a 5-8% return for most portfolios over the course of 15 years, so saving $18,000 to $23,000 or better yet, maxing out your tax advantaged retirement savings accounts should be your if you have put off saving for your retirement.

SPENDING DOWN YOUR RETIREMENT SAVINGS

Albert C. Wong writes, "Transitioning to the phase for diligent savers can be a tricky time. After all, the very personality features that led you to save for more than

40 years don't just go away when it's time to draw down your assets. The goal is to be able to shift from a saving to a mindset by evaluating the impact of spending decisions against their family and their long-term financial success. Focusing on how your spending matches your values helps you realize that building lasting family in your retirement is one of the reasons you saved so hard in the first place."

"Spending from what seems to be a pool of non replenishing resources can make you worry about 'opportunity costs'—other ways you could be your money or the trade-off of spending those resources today. Being focused on the long-term and taking a approach to investing are core investing principles. But if you're in a good financial position, there comes a time when it's okay to live out the retirement you have spent your planning for. Family memories are priceless."

RE-EVALUATING THE 4% DRAWDOWN RULE

Patrick Villanova writes, "The 4% Rule has for a long time been considered a way to draw down your savings in retirement. Developed in 1994 by financial planner William Bengen, the 4% Rule has become a staple of retirement planning. Bengen was able to mathematically demonstrate that a whose portfolio is 50:50 stocks/bonds can initially withdraw 4% of their retirement savings and then adjust future withdrawals for inflation."

"Recently Morningstar researchers found this often-cited rule of thumb needs some updating. The financial services firm found that retirees seeking a withdrawal strategy that will produce 30 years of retirement income should start by withdrawing % of their savings. Morningstar researchers say that the current bond yields and an equity (stock) market that is likely are the primary reasons a 4% withdrawal rate 'may no longer be feasible.'"

"Flexible spend down strategies whose withdrawal rates on a yearly basis can ensure retirees don't overspend in periods of market and provide more income in stronger economic environments. One method that will mitigate the chance of running out of money in retirement is to the inflation adjustments after a year in which your portfolio in value. A retiree using this approach could safely withdraw 3.76% of their savings in the first year and still have a 90% chance of having money left over after 30 years."

"A second method of spend down strategy is to use what is referred to as the Guardrail Method. In addition to adjusting for inflation, the Guardrail Method establishes for how much a withdrawal rate can increase during times of market strength, and how much it can during economic downturns. With a portfolio comprising 50% equities and 50% bonds, a retiree could start by withdrawing 4.72% and then set parameters for how low or high the rate can go depending on portfolio . Morningstar found this method "does the best job of payouts in a safe and livable way."

"Another spend-down strategy Morningstar looked at was to reduce the portfolio withdrawal rate by % after portfolio losses. Similar to the first alternative strategy, this method relies on reacting to losing years. Retirees using this strategy would their withdrawal rate by 10% after years in which the portfolio declines in value. This approach produced an initial withdrawal rate of 3.57%, slightly higher than the 3.3% suggested for a fixed-rate strategy. This approach also resulted in the largest median ending portfolio after 30 years, making it the best option for retirees who have a younger spouse or who are motivated by leaving a to family."

INVESTING DURING RETIREMENT

Coryanne Hicks writes, "Investing during retirement is anything but straightforward. Retirees have to juggle finding safe investments to their income streams while not being so safe they risk their money in retirement."

"It is even more important in retirement to be mindful of your risks. Consider the different experience of an accumulating investor versus a decumulating investor during a down market. While the accumulating investor considers a market a sale on stocks because they have the ability to purchase more shares at lower prices, the decumulating retiree may be to sell their shares at lower than desired prices to fund their retirement needs. For this reason, retirees need to make sure they aren't taking on too much risk, with money they'll need in the next couple of years."

"Inflation during retirement can create another type of for retirees: The risk of running out of money in retirement. Inflation can cause you to burn through your retirement savings faster than if you don't take measures to mitigate the corrosion. For current retirees who are seeing increases in food, gas, energy, and other consumer goods prices, they can try to offset this inflationary environment by investing in I-Bonds or increasing their (stock) position in their portfolio to help lessen the impact of rising prices."

"Retirees need to balance their portfolio to a 'just right' investment strategy that is able to provide their retirement income needs while not investing for a rate of return than their retirement needs. In order to keep your retirement risk in perspective, it may be wise to the money you need to fund your retirement, from the assets you want to accumulate and pass on as a legacy. This way you can grow the assets you do not for retirement without risking your future security."

A recent study done by Fidelity Investments determined that a better long-term strategy of withdrawals for overall tax consequences was to withdraw an equal amount out of all types of retirement accounts (taxable, tax-deferred, and Roth IRA).

TURN INVESTMENT / WITHDRAWALS IN RETIREMENT INTO 5 YEAR PERIODS

Coryanne Hicks writes, "It may be wise to break your retirement spending needs into five-year segments. No one single investment or investment style (i.e. asset allocation) can address the of a 30 year retirement. Each five year segment of retirement has its own unique needs and therefore investment needs. Money invested during the first two or three segments (five years prior to retirement and 5-10 years following retirement need to be invested more than money invested later in retirement years. The reason for this is during this pre and early retirement period your retirement income needs are highly affected by the stock and bond markets of returns, meaning that large losses during this period could negatively affect your portfolio's ability to provide you with income throughout your lifetime. Withdrawing income from an investment portfolio during a market decline removes that will never be replaced again. Five year investment segments from 11 through 25 years can be invested for since they'll have time to recover from negative or bear markets."

A GUARANTEED INCOME IMMEDIATE LIFETIME ANNUITY

Consider adding a Guaranteed Income Immediate Lifetime Annuity as insurance against an apocalyptic stock market or another decade during your retirement years. Annuities have gotten a bad rap as fee-heavy products, but they can serve the savvy retiree well. This asset can essentially, along with Social Security, essentially much of what used to be allocated to bonds, and the payouts are usually much higher. Although you give up some liquidity, they can pay very high guaranteed incomes and run out for you and your spouse's lifetime.

"Our salvation is now than when we first believed." ROMANS 13:11

TAX ADVANTAGED CHARITABLE DONATIONS

Taylor Turner writes, "Giving to charities that are important to us is a profoundly and emotional act. It is rewarding to help individuals, our places of worship, communities, and causes we care about. Building a formal plan of giving and updating it each year can help you meet your charitable goals while maximizing tax savings. Consider these long-term strategies to make the most of your charitable giving."

"Donate appreciated instead of cash. Giving appreciated assets, such as stocks (or stock funds) means more money going to charities and to taxes. You won't have to pay capital gains taxes when you donate an appreciated asset, and charities don't have to pay taxes when they sell them. You'll still receive a deduction, and you'll meet your giving goals—possibly having paid less out of pocket."

DONOR-ADVISED FUNDS

"Using a Donor-Advised Fund is a great way to contributions and spread out distributions over time." "Bunch your contributions to maximize deductions on your return. Planning ahead and itemizing your deductions may be a choice." You can 'bunch' your contributions for charitable giving for more than one year, into one year if it yields a higher tax benefit.

QUALIFIED CHARITABLE DISTRIBUTIONS (QCDs)

"If you are 73 years old or older, consider using Qualified Charitable Distributions. If you're not itemizing your deductions and you're at the Required Minimum Distribution (RMD) age of 73 (this age is going up to 75 in the next few years), you may want to consider donating part of your RMD to a charity through a QCD. It'll satisfy your RMD, and up to $100,000 annually won't count as taxable income."

LEAVING A BEQUEST

"Finally, you can name a charity as a beneficiary or leave a bequest in your will or trust. Look at this as a of giving. Naming a charity as a beneficiary or leaving a bequest in your will or trust allows you to give to causes that are meaningful to you without possibly yourself if you would happen to need to spend late in life on long-term care or health expenses. Charitable bequests are eligible for the estate tax and can reduce estate taxes."

"I tell you, use worldly to gain friends for yourselves, so that when it is gone, you will be welcomed into eternal dwellings." LUKE 16:9

CONCLUSION

Defining your purpose in retirement life is key to retirement happiness or joy. Determine if you are ready to retire by knowing your financial numbers! Determine your optimal claiming age for Social Security. Use a life expectancy calculator to help determine an approximate longevity to your life and that of your spouse, to help determine if your retirement funds will last you and your spouse's lifetimes. If you are late to retirement savings, maximize your retirement contributions. Plan for the decumulation period of spending down your retirement savings by withdrawing 3.3 to 4 percent per year with a cost of inflation adjustment each year. Use a Donor-Advised Fund to bunch charitable contributions, or Qualified Charitable Distributions to help meet your RMD after age 73, as this will not count as taxable income.

LESSON 15

INSURANCE: DEFENDING AGAINST FINANCIAL DISASTER

"A catastrophe you cannot foresee will suddenly come upon you."
ISAIAH 45:7

"Watch out that you do not lose what we have worked for, but that you may be rewarded fully."
2 JOHN 1:8

HOW DOES INSURANCE WORK FOR EVERYBODY

Insurance is your way of transferring __________ from you to an insurance company. You don't want to be one of the uninsured when the __________ happens.

"What I __________ has come upon me; what I dreaded has happened to me. I have no __________, no quietness; I have no rest; but only turmoil." JOB 3:25-26

The insurance company uses actuarial data using all kinds of __________ including your age, your claims history, where you live, pre-existing conditions, how many miles you drive per year, the effect of weather patterns, whether you are bundling different types of coverage, to determine your insurance __________ (the amount you have to pay for the coverage you have chosen). By combining your risk with the risk of __________ other policyholders, the insurance company softens the blow of paying out any given insurance claim.

The premium you pay is also determined by the __________ you choose. The deductible is the amount you personally must pay, prior to the insurance paying their share of the claim. Choosing a higher deductible (i.e. $500 or $1000) will decrease the premium you will be required to pay. If you have a fully funded emergency fund, raising your deductible would be a __________ way of saving money on your premiums on the front end. You should not make any claim to your insurance company for any damage that is __________ your deductible. Repeated claims under a particular policy will result in a __________ insurance premium. Just pay to get the repair completed, in cash, by using your emergency fund.

You can find insurance coverage for almost any type of loss you can imagine.

"Disaster will come upon __________, and you will not know how to conjure it away. A calamity will fall upon you that you cannot ward off with a __________; a catastrophe you cannot foresee will __________ come upon you." ISAIAH 47:11

You only want to insure against the large financial losses that may occur, the types of events that will severely __________ your financial health. We are going to examine the rationale for maintaining insurance coverage in the following categories: Health, Auto, Homeowners/Renters, Catastrophe, Disability, Life, Long-term Care, and Umbrella Liability.

HEALTH INSURANCE

Health Insurance is a necessity given that an ________ resulting in physical harm can happen to all of us without notice. That, of course, is why they call them accidents! If health insurance is offered at your work you want to take advantage of this benefit in order to be part of the ________, and as such pay lower premiums. If both you and your spouse are offered health insurance benefits, determine if each should stay on their own company plan or which plan gives you the best "________ for your buck." Add dependents to the plan that makes the most sense for both coverage and economics.

There are basically two types of health insurance coverage. A ________ Deductible Health Plan with an HSA (Health Savings Account) or plans with lower deductibles that the insurance company pays a ________ of the costs (i.e. 90/10, 80/20, 70/30) where the insurance company will pay 90% and you pay 10% of the claim after your deductible is met. You'll have to run the numbers, based on your family's particular health care ________, but oftentimes the 80/20 Policy is the "sweet spot" for ________ when it comes to upfront cost with adequate coverage. This policy would pay after the deductible 80% of the claim, while you as the policyholder would pay 20% of the claim.

HIGH-DEDUCTIBLE HEALTH PLAN WITH HSA

A High-Deductible Health Plan with a Health Savings Account (HSA) may be the best choice for the ________ and healthy. This is the type of plan to choose if you don't anticipate any health care ________, because with the high deductible, you will be paying for most of your health care costs out of pocket up front, by using money placed in your HSA. The advantage of this plan comes with the HSA which is triple ________ advantaged. The money you place in this account goes in pre-tax, the money ________ in the account tax free, and can be withdrawn without tax if used for a ________ expense any time in the future. Many employers will place money for you into your HSA each year you enroll in the High-Deductible Plan. If you are young, healthy, and risk ________ this may help you build health savings for use in future years, and maybe into retirement when towards the end of your life you'll need significant resources to cover anticipated health care costs.

HEALTH INSURANCE: FLEXIBLE SPENDING ACCOUNT

If a High Deductible Health Plan is NOT right for you or your family based on a higher ________ for health care services, consider using a Flexible Spending Account (FSA) to save on your health care costs. The Flexible ________ Account allows you to withdraw from your paycheck pre-tax for authorized health care expenses, saving you the amount of your ________ bracket on these purchases. Authorized healthcare expenses can include visit copays, prescription medications, healthcare bills such as medical imaging or lab tests not covered by insurance, and some durable medical equipment and Over-The-Counter medications.

AUTO INSURANCE

If you own a car, auto insurance is a must! In fact, many states you to carry liability and personal injury protection. Let's go through the types of auto insurance coverage available, and what each part of the policy covers. When it comes to liability coverage the policy is written with three numbers. The first number covers injuries to individual involved in the accident, the second number is the total amount per accident payed out in claims, and the third number covers damage to covered per accident (each of these numbers is expressed in multiples of a thousand dollars).

Rivan Stinson writes, "Let's look at what a good liability policy might look like. Let's say that you have a 100/300/100 auto liability policy. This means you have coverage up to $100,000 per of individual injury coverage, up to a $300,000 maximum per accident of all individual's injury coverage, and up to $100,000 of personal property , to prevent being sued for the difference of what your policy covers, and the damage to the other vehicles involved if you are determined responsible for the accident."

Ramsey Solutions write, "Personal Injury Protection (PIP) is a specific type of auto insurance that covers hospital bills, medical costs, and a loss of wages if you get injured in a car accident. It is also called no-fault protection because it doesn't matter who is at fault—you're covered." "PIP must be exhausted before your health insurance policy will cover medical after a motor vehicle accident." "Be aware that your insurer may have a strict process about when you must a claim after an accident for PIP coverage to apply."

"Collision and Comprehensive coverage are usually bundled under an auto insurance policy. Collision insurance covers damage caused when the driver with something while comprehensive coverage generally covers events that are of the driver's control. Comprehensive coverage (covers damage to your car such as)...a natural disaster, theft, damage from striking an animal, vandalism, an act of terrorism, or a falling object. The main benefit of comprehensive insurance is to give you peace of mind and financial protection if something really happens to your car." "Having these coverages along with required liability and PIP is considered full-coverage."

If you have a car loan, lease, or if your vehicle's value is more than you can replace without completely decimating your emergency fund, I recommend carrying comprehensive and collision insurance. Rivan Stinson writes, "However, for older cars, the amount of coverage you need comes down to math. If the value of your car is worth less than what you're paying in annual premiums the deductibles, then it may be time to drop collision and possibly comprehensive coverage, too. To check the value of your car, go to www.kbb.com or www.edmunds.com and type in your vehicle information." "Both sites will give a range of estimates based on your car's condition. If you're still not convinced that dropping coverage is worth it, ask your insurance company for different quote combinations." My personal rule for dropping coverage is: You own your car , your car has very high miles (i.e. 250,000+ miles on the odometer), it has a very low value (i.e.<=$3,000), and you can easily afford to replace it.

HOMEOWNERS / RENTERS INSURANCE

Homeowners insurance is financial protection for your home and __________ belongings in the case of accidents, fires, or other disasters.

"Disaster follows disaster…In an instant my tents (________) are destroyed, my shelter in a moment." JEREMIAH 4:20

It's a way of transferring risk to an insurance company to avoid financially disastrous events. Homeowners insurance also protects you from lawsuits due to accidents ____ your property.

For most people their home is their __________ investment. Knowing the basics of coverage is the first step toward getting the right amount of coverage. Your insurance declaration page will give you a breakdown of your __________ homeowners policy.

"Dwelling" coverage pays to repair or rebuild your house and anything __________ to it due to damage from disasters such as: fire, windstorms, hail, lightning, tornadoes, theft and vandalism.

"And fire, which __________ says, 'Enough.'" PROVERBS 30:16

"But understand this: If the owner of the house had __________ at what time of night the thief was coming, he would have kept watch and would not have let his house be broken into." MATTHEW 24:43 / LUKE 12:39

If you live in a coastal area that gets hit by hurricanes, dwelling coverage won't cover wind or __________ damage. You need separate policies for hurricane coverage or flood damage.

"'Other structures' coverage covers things other than your house. Some examples of 'other structures' include: Detached garage, tool shed, barn, gazebo, swimming pool, fence, and driveway. There are __________ to how much the insurance company will pay to repair or replace these structures—usually around ____ % of the total policy you have on your home. Different policies cover different structures, so make sure the structures on your property are __________ covered in your policy."

"'Personal property' coverage protects what is ____ your home. It covers things like clothes, furniture and electronics…There is also a dollar ________ attached to personal property to replace damaged or stolen valuables. Most insurance companies will cover your belongings around __________ % of what your home is valued at. To make sure your stuff is actually covered, go through your house and take an __________ of everything. So get out a clipboard and make a paper record, or use your phone to do a video log, and take a few hours to inventory your stuff.

"'Personal liability' coverage is one of the best types of homeowners insurance coverage you can buy. It protects you from __________ for bodily injury, property damage that occurs on your property and depending on the breed of dog, even dog bites. The good news is that the insurance company will pay for legal representation and cover the damage if you are found __________ for the accident. More good news is that personal liability coverage doesn't cost much. You should carry at least $500,000 in liability, and if you have a larger Net Worth, you should probably have an __________ insurance policy to protect yourself."

"The guilty party must pay the injured person for any ________ of time and see that the victim is completely healed." EXODUS 21:19

"'Additional Living Expense' (ALE) coverage will help you pay for the expenses of living from home due to damage from an insured disaster. That includes things like bills, restaurant meals, pet care, transportation, and even moving expenses if you're out of your home for a while. ALE won't pay for your expenses, it only kicks in for costs that are above and regular living expenses. ALE has limits, usually around 20% of your dwelling coverage."

Catastrophe Insurance is a type of insurance that protects your home from natural disasters such as floods, hurricanes, earthquakes, tornadoes, volcanoes, and sinkholes. Some homeowners, who live in areas that could be subject to wildfires, would be wise to purchase separate fire insurance policies for extended coverage of their home and belongings.

"In that day they will ask, 'Have not these come on us because our God is not with us?'"
DEUTERONOMY 31:17

If you live in an area where any of these types of disasters are a possibility, you should strongly consider purchasing a Catastrophe Insurance rider.

HOMEOWNERS INSURANCE

The price of Homeowners Insurance has increased by ~20% in the past few years due to increasing claims for related damage. The cost of homeowners insurance ranges widely depending on such things like where you live, the of your home, your past history of homeowners insurance claims, your score, level of coverage, and whether you need extras like flood or hurricane insurance.

RENTERS INSURANCE

Renters insurance is a necessity to cover your if you rent or lease a home or an apartment. In the case of a fire, smoke damage, damage from automated sprinklers, or other natural disasters the only way your belongings will be covered is if you have insurance. Purchase renters insurance if you are not the homeowner.

SHORT-TERM DISABILITY INSURANCE

Guardian Life Insurance Company of America reports, "Each year, over 5% of American workers will experience a short-term due to illness, injury, or pregnancy. Disability often results in lost income and medical expenses that can throw your financial plans track. That's why short-term disability insurance coverage is a vital protection to help ensure an illness or injury won't damage your personal financial plan." "Statistically, 1 in (25%) of today's 20 year olds will become before they retire."

"Disability insurance is sometimes referred to as replacement because it pays you benefits to replace a portion of the income you lose if you're unable to work due to a prolonged illness or injury. Short-term disability insurance typically starts to pay benefits within two weeks of a illness or injury and covers you for a benefit period that's usually between 13-26 weeks, and typically replaces from 40-70% of your income during the ______ period…Cancer, pregnancy, mental health issues and musculoskeletal diseases are among the top reasons for disability claims." "Plan to select short-term disability coverage that will cover you during the ______ period, or 'elimination period' in your long-term disability policy."

LONG-TERM DISABILITY INSURANCE

"As the name implies Long-Term Disability Insurance is income replacement coverage for a more extended recovery from approved disability situations. It pays you benefits to replace a portion of the income you lose if you're ______ to work due to a prolonged illness or injury. You will receive benefits until you are able to ______ to work or until you reach the end of your benefit period. To claim benefits you'll need to submit a claim along with information about your condition from your ______. If your claim is approved, you'll start to receive benefits determined by your plan as soon as the waiting period has passed. The money is paid to you directly, and there is no limitation on ______ it can be spent. Since Social Security disability benefits are typically less than your regular income, it's important to have additional protections in place to help ensure your finances can stay on track if you experience an ______ illness or injury."

"Depending on how your policy is written, disability insurance can replace up to ______ % of your pre-tax income following a waiting period (elimination period) usually of 3 months. Your benefit period can last 5, 10, or 20 years, or until you reach retirement, depending on the ______ of the policy.

LIFE INSURANCE

One of the best ways to protect those who ______ on your income for financial stability is Life Insurance. If you are buying Life Insurance for the first time, there are a few things you can do to make the process easier.

"Now listen, you who say, 'Today or tomorrow we will go to this or that city, spend a year there, carry on business and make money.' Why, you do not even ______ what will happen tomorrow. What is your life? You are a mist that appears for a ______ while and then vanishes. Instead you ought to say, 'If it is the ______ will, we will live and do this or that.'" JAMES 4:13-15

"No one has power over the ______ of their death." ECCLESIASTES 8:8

The first thing to do is get a ______ picture of your finances including your assets, emergency fund, and financial obligations. You might want to consider purchasing enough life insurance to pay off your mortgage, put your kids through college or your ______ replacement for supporting your spouse. You're looking to acquire enough life insurance coverage that will give you peace of mind while providing financial ______ for your family.

You want to buy Term Life Insurance, which expires after a set ______ of years, usually 5, 10, 15, 20 or 30 years. Term life Insurance is much ______ expensive than Whole Life Insurance, and is a better choice to help keep ______ low. You want to avoid purchasing a Whole Life or Universal Life

Insurance policy as it is much wiser to separate out your insurance coverage from your investments. Take the money you save when buying Term Life Insurance and it wisely, and you'll find yourself far ahead of where you would have been due to the underlying costs of Whole Life and Universal Life insurance.

Your health and are the most important factors companies take into account when giving you a life insurance quote. The younger you are, the more likely you are to pay a lower premium. Unhealthy habits or disease that will increase your chance of an early demise could lead to higher rates.

"One person dies in full vigor, completely and at ease." JOB 21:23

While your monthly cost, the , is often one of the biggest factors to consider, but it's not the only thing to think about. It is always wise to check the company you're considering purchasing a policy from for longevity and stability.

Life insurance is the best way to protect your loved ones in the event you have an death. If you are single, you DO NOT need life insurance. If you have sufficient financial assets for your family to continue on hardship, you DO NOT need life insurance.

"The of the rich is their fortified city; they imagine it a wall too high to scale." PROVERBS 18:11

MoneyTalksNews Staff writes, "For everybody else, term life insurance that will provide you with the coverage you need, at a price you can afford, is a must for financial , and peace of mind for your family. While the Forbes Advisor gives us this advice, "Rule of Thumb: Most financial planners recommend you consider purchasing 10- times your current annual income in life insurance.

"The ransom for life is , no payment is ever enough." PSALM 48:8

LONG-TERM CARE INSURANCE

Figuring out the sweet spot on purchasing Long-Term Care Insurance is one of the most complicated of all insurance types to compare rates. And Long-Term Care Insurance is and getting more expensive every year.

Did you know that a 65 year old today has a % chance of needing some type of long-term care? Around 20% will need it longer than 5 years. Having a Long-term Care Insurance Policy will take away a ton of about your future. It'll also ease the burden off your loved ones.

You basically have two choices: You can either sock that money away and it over the next 25-30 years, so you can afford to pay any necessary long-term care expenses out of pocket, or you can pay an insurance company a to do the same and provide you with the contractual benefits.

Long-Term Care Insurance is a policy that covers costs related to caretakers who come to your home for care, assisted facilities, or nursing home care. It pays for support for those who can no longer perform out of six everyday activities of daily living. Since long-term care costs are not covered by regular health insurance, Medicare, and only for certain long-term care expenses under Medicaid, the government program for low income people, that's where the need for long-term care insurance comes into play in a well financial plan.

Ramsey Solutions writes, "The average cost of a semi-private nursing home stay in the United States is $7,756/month, and that rises to $8,821/month for a private room. The estimated costs for care in the final five years of life is $367,000 for people with dementia and $234,000 for those without. On Americans pay a total of $172,000 for long-term care. And keep in mind these costs are rising year over year. If you don't have a solid plan, these costs could burn up your pretty quickly.

According to federal data, women men by about 5 years and need an average of 3.7 years of care as opposed to only 2.2 years of care for the average man.

Most policies are written with a 90 day waiting before insurance kicks in. This means you should have savings of about months worth of nursing home care set aside to fill this gap, even with Long-Term Care Insurance in place. In order for your Long-Term Care policy to keep pace with the costs of care you should add a % inflation rider.

Although Long-term Care Insurance is expensive, your premiums are tax up to a certain limit. Be sure to ask your insurance agent prior to buying if your Long-term Care premiums are tax as deductible.

The Maximum Amount of Premiums You Can Tax Deduct Based on Age (2025)

Age 51-60	$1800
Age 61-70	$4810
Age 71+	$6020

HYBRID LONG-TERM CARE INSURANCE

Hybrid Long-term Care policies are a combination of insurance with long-term care coverage. They allow your beneficiary to receive a benefit, equal to your premiums paid, if you don't end up needing long-term care. Hybrid policies are typically more expensive than traditional long-term care policies. While hybrid policy premiums are fixed, they're tax deductible.

It is recommended you apply for Long-Term Care Insurance at the age of , before you may acquire any health concerns that may eliminate you from being approved for a Long-Term Care Insurance policy.

"Very truly I tell you, when you were younger you dressed and went where you wanted; but when you are you will stretch out your hands, and someone else will dress you and you where you do not want to go." JOHN 21:18

UMBRELLA LIABILITY INSURANCE

As your financial plan comes to fruition, and your assets grow, you should strongly consider Umbrella Liability coverage. Umbrella insurance is coverage that provides protection beyond the existing limits and coverages of motor vehicle and homeowners policies. Umbrella insurance can provide coverage for injuries, property damage, certain lawsuits, and liability situations.

"Any man or woman who another in any way...must confess the sin they have committed. They must make restitution for the wrong they have done." NUMBERS 5:6-7

McKayla Girardin writes, "Umbrella insurance is fairly inexpensive and is worth it if the value of your exceeds your auto or home liability insurance , and for those who have a Net Worth of at least $500,000. This type of insurance is relatively inexpensive because it supplements other policies, and because it covers circumstances that are unlikely. The rule of thumb for umbrella insurance is to buy as much coverage as your total , factoring in assets like your home, car, investments, and even your retirement accounts."

"An umbrella policy protects your assets against the cost of losing a lawsuit over a car accident, a boating accident if you carry liability insurance on your boat, or an accident on your property. Since individuals with a moderate or high net worth can be a for lawsuits, purchasing umbrella insurance can keep your assets from being seized if a liability judgment against you exceeds your home or car insurance limits. As a result, it's a good idea to err on the side of caution and purchase umbrella coverage rather than less."

CONCLUSION

Insurance coverage is a necessary defense against financial disaster. Depending on your current financial circumstances, you should consider appropriate insurance coverage for your unique situation to protect yourself and family against a catastrophic financial event. As people of faith, you can be sure that the LORD knows each and every circumstance that we may encounter, and He is preparing us to walk through whatever challenges life may bring. Remember the words of Deuteronomy 31:8 when it says, "The LORD Himself goes before you and will be with you; He will never leave you nor forsake you. Do not be afraid; do not be discouraged."

ACTION STEPS

1. When was the last time you reviewed your insurance protection?

If it has been more than 3-5 years, schedule a meeting with your insurance agent.

2. Do you have adequate life insurance to protect your family?

Review your current policy, and purchase any term life insurance necessary to provide adequate protection.

3. Have you accumulated enough assets (Net Worth) that an umbrella policy would be a good idea?

LESSON 16

TAXES AND YOUR FINANCES

"They came to Him (Jesus) and said, 'Teacher, we know You are a man of integrity. You aren't swayed by others, because You pay no attention to who they are; but you teach the way of God in accordance with the truth. Is it right to pay the imperial tax to Caesar or not?' … 'Bring me a denarius and let me look at it.' They brought the coin, and He asked them, 'Whose portrait is this?' 'Caesars,' they replied. Then Jesus said to them, 'Give to Caesar what is Caesar's, and to God what is God's.'"

MARK 12:14-17 MATTHEW 22:17-21 LUKE 20:21-25

DISCLAIMER

Please do not consider any of the following information to be investment or advice. You must do your own due and consult an investment professional like a CFP (Certified Financial Planner) and/or a CPA (Certified Public Accountant) for up to date tax advice.

WHAT IS THE TAX STRUCTURE OF YOUR PORTFOLIO?

William J Bernstein writes, "The key question is, what is the tax structure of your portfolio? ...Many professionals have most of their portfolio in 401k, IRA, Keogh, and pension accounts. This gives them the freedom to invest in almost asset class they desire without to tax consequences."

While Kathleen Coxwell reports the importance of minimizing taxes when she writes, "Yes, you'll still pay taxes in retirement…The average American family pays about $10,500 a year in total income taxes, including federal, state and local taxes. Ten thousand dollars can be a big of change, being about 14% of the average retirement budget." "Tax planning should be a part of your retirement plan. Forethought can help you much more of your hard earned money. When studied it was found that for a typical couple in retirement, the effective tax rate dramatically—between zero and 23.8%—and there was no single number you could choose to give the correct answer over an retirement! Even more alarming is that estimates suggest that for each 1% error in effective tax rate, you introduce an % error in your final retirement savings balance."

THE IMPORTANCE OF TAX EFFICIENCY IN INVESTING

William J Bernstein writes, "Tax-efficiency is an extremely concept to understand. It is a measure of the percent of a fund's return you receive after the taxes on the distributions are paid." "A stock fund with no turnover (i.e. index) will produce no capital-gains distributions; you will be taxed only on the relatively amount of stock dividends the fund passes through to you. Such a fund is tax-efficient." "On the other hand, an managed stock fund with high turnover will periodically distribute a large amount of capital gains to you, on which taxes be paid. Such a fund is tax-inefficient. Worst of all are REIT and junk bond funds, which distribute almost all their return in the form of . Further, these dividends are taxed at the high ordinary income rate. Obviously, then, you will want to hold only tax-efficient funds in your taxable account, reserving the most tax-inefficient ones for your retirement (tax-sheltered) accounts." "Since tax-efficient equity (stock) funds provide excellent deferral of taxation, the all-taxable investor will want a portion of stocks, than the all-sheltered investor, all other things being equal."

WHY YOU SHOULD PAY YOUR TAXES

God's word says in Romans 13:1 that "Everyone must himself to the governing authorities, for there is no authority except that which is established . The authorities that exist have been established by God." God establishes it is our duty as citizens to pay our taxes. Jesus says in Matthew 22:21 "give to Caesar (the government) what is Caesar's, and to God what is God's." In Romans 13:6-7 it states, "This is also why you taxes, for the authorities are God's servants, who give their full to governing. Give everyone what you him: If you owe taxes, pay taxes; if revenue, then revenue; if respect, then respect; if honor then honor."

This does not mean we need to pay more than our fair share of taxes. In Luke 3:13 John the Baptizer said to the tax collectors, "Don't collect any more than you are required to." We may minimize our taxes by using any wise methods that are legally and permissible.

TAX ADVANTAGED OR TAX SHELTERED SAVINGS

It is wise to use tax advantaged savings for our retirement savings, whether a 401(k), 403(b), Traditional IRA, Roth IRA, or Roth 401(k). These are all tax advantaged savings programs authorized by the that will reduce your in the present or in the future.

Andrew Tobias writes, "The basic difference between the Roth IRA and the Traditional IRA is that with the Traditional one you get your tax break on the way (contributions are made pre-tax)...whereas with the Roth IRA you get your break on the way (contributions are made with after tax money, and your earnings and withdrawals are tax free)." The same is true when considering the 401(k) (or 403b) the money goes into the investment account - , and this money is taxed upon withdrawal and is subject to Minimum Distributions (RMDs) after age 73. While with a Roth 401(k) the money is invested taxes and is not taxed upon withdrawal, although it is subject to RMDs.

TAX ADVANTAGED OR TAX SHELTERED SAVINGS

Andrew Tobias writes, "If you want to retire in comfort, we will have to provide, in measure (plus Social Security), for ourselves. Fortunately, there are a variety of tax-deferred retirement plans to help." "The best retirement plans are the 401(k) and 403(b) 'salary reduction plans'...What makes them so good is that many employers add 25 cents or 50 cents or even more to each dollar you to save this way. This is free money." "You should fund your 401(k)...because:

- It is a relatively painless way to save.
- You avoid taxes on the money you contribute until, many years later, (when) you withdraw it.
- In the meantime, no tax is due as it grows.

Kathleen Coxwell writes, "The Roth IRA is popular because your money grows tax free, are not taxed, and you are not required to take minimum distributions. In 2024, you can only save into a Roth IRA if your modified adjusted gross income (MAGI)is $161,000 or less as a single filer, or $240,000 or less as a married couple filing jointly. Tax-free is the name of the Roth IRA game...so invest for growth appropriate for your age, time horizon, and risk tolerance."

DON'T OVERLOOK THE OPPORTUNITY FOR YOUR SPOUSE TO SAVE

If your spouse has earned income, make sure they are saving in the most advantageous vehicles possible, which may very well be a IRA account. Even if your spouse does not have earned income, you can max out a Roth IRA by using a IRA. No financial decision should ever be made without understanding the pros and cons in terms of both your and future overall financial picture. Investors in an IRA or 401(k) account need not burden their nor their checkbooks with tax issues. As taxes are deferred, returns rise significantly with each additional year that an investor elects to fund shares.

The Jeffrey Company says, "Taxable is a loser's game. Those who lose the least—taxes and fees—stand to win the most when the game is over." To put it simply: A tax that is deferred is the functional equivalent of an interest-free from the U.S. Treasury Department, with a maturity equal to the number of years of deferral.

WHAT THE BIBLE SAYS REGARDING TAXES

"But when the crop comes in, give a of it to Pharaoh. The other four-fifths you may keep as seed for the fields and as for yourselves and your households and your children." GENESIS 47:24-25

"He taxed the land and exacted the silver and gold from the people of the land to their assessment." 2 KINGS 23:35

Taxes were here from the beginning and will be until Christ returns!

DO NOT USE ACTIVELY MANAGED FUNDS IN TAXABLE ACCOUNTS

Actively managed mutual funds routinely ignore taxes, by engaging in rapid-fire portfolio transaction activity (portfolio turnover), which generates taxes for investors using taxable accounts. The dichotomy is that a portfolio manager's performance is measured and applauded on the basis of pretax return...Few portfolio managers spend their time agonizing over the tax of their decisions (portfolio turnover). Transaction costs are considerably more in international markets, thus the annual to be overcome by active managers approaches 4 percent, nearly double the plus 2 percent handicap faced by U.S. equity managers…A much needed prospectus of full disclosure of actively managed funds should read: This fund is managed without regard to tax considerations, and given its expected rate of portfolio turnover, is likely to realize and a high portion of its capital returns in the form of capital gains that are taxable annually, a substantial portion of which are likely to realized in the form of short-term gains subject to income tax rates.

INDEX MUTUAL FUNDS ARE TAX EFFICIENT

The index fund is the odds-on favorite to outpace of every four mutual fund managers. An investor's goal is not simply to minimize the tax burden, but rather to achieve the highest possible returns. The annual portfolio turnover of an all-market index fund rarely exceeds 2-3 percent, essentially for an average holding period of 33 to 50 years. That long time horizon is surely a significant factor in the formidable relative pre-tax returns that index funds have provided, as well as in their almost unparalleled in providing after-tax returns. The bottom line is index mutual funds are tax efficient.

We suggest that the best solution to this problem in taxable accounts is to use low-cost, low-turnover, tax-efficient funds that do not depend on the skill, or luck, of stock-picking managers. They are tax efficient and low cost, reflect their benchmark index, and can be indefinitely.

The lower tax rates on qualified dividends increase the tax-efficiency of holding stocks to bonds, in taxable accounts, whose yield is taxed at ordinary income tax rates. We generally recommend placing stocks in taxable accounts and in tax-advantaged accounts.

BUY AND HOLD TO AVOID SHORT-TERM CAPITAL GAINS TAXES

A short-term capital gain is a profit on the sale of a security or mutual fund share that is held for 12 months or less. A long-term capital gain is a profit on the sale of a security or mutual fund share that is held for than one year. One of the easiest and most effective ways to cut mutual fund taxes significantly is to hold mutual funds for more than 12 months. Buy-and-hold is a very effective strategy in accounts.

INVESTMENTS AND THEIR TAX EFFICIENCY

For maximum tax efficiency in taxable accounts, you should do the following.

1. Favor funds with low dividends
2. Favor funds with "qualified" dividends
3. Favor fund with low turnover
4. Favor tax-efficient index funds and tax managed funds

RELATIVE TAX EFFICIENCY RANKINGS

The relative tax efficiency rankings for major classes from the most tax efficient to least tax efficient is:

1. Low yielding cash, money market funds
2. Tax managed stock funds
3. Total market stock index funds
4. Mid-cap and small-cap index funds
5. Active stock funds
6. Balanced funds
7. Taxable bond funds
8. REIT funds
9. High yield bond funds

A good source for locating a fund's tax efficiency rating is www.morningstar.com. Morningstar provides a "Tax-Cost Ratio," which is the actual percentage point reduction in return resulting from taxes for an investor in the federal tax bracket. Use the Ratio from the longest period so that both bull and bear market cycles are included.

PORTFOLIO TAX MANAGEMENT

Tax manage your own portfolio by:

1. Keeping turnover low—buy funds and hold forever
2. Use only tax-efficient funds in taxable accounts
3. Avoid short-term capital gains—hold profitable shares longer than 12 months
4. Buy fund shares after the distribution date
5. Sell fund shares before the distribution date
6. Sell profitable shares after the New Year
7. Harvest tax losses to reduce current and future income taxes

MAX YOUR TAX-ADVANTAGED ACCOUNTS PRIOR TO TAXABLE ACCOUNT

Ben Carlson writes, "Anyone starting out saving should have as much of their long-term capital as possible in tax accounts. This is a no-brainer for those funds you won't need to touch for decades." "Bonds, REITS, high dividend-paying stocks, and pretty much anything with regular payments besides tax-free municipal bonds, should go in tax-deferred retirement accounts because they are tax inefficient assets.

"You can max out your elective deferral contributions to 401(k), 403(b), 457 and Thrift Savings plans up to $23,500/year. If you are over 50 you can use a - contribution of $7,500 for a total savings of up to $31,000/year. The contribution limit for Traditional and Roth IRAs is $7,000, with a catch-up contribution of an additional $1000 for a total of $8,000 for those 50 and older."

DEDUCTIONS THAT SAVE ON YOUR TAXES

Know that if you are 65 or older you have a higher Standard Deduction. In 2025:

Singles	$17,000
Married (filing jointly with both over 65)	$33,200
Head of Household	$24,500

You can put money into a Health Savings Account (HSA) to increase your tax deductions as long as a High Deductible Health Plan is medical insurance for you and your family. Money put in an HSA is deductible up to $4,150 for individuals and $8,300 for families in 2024—plus an additional $1,000 if you are over age 55. Distributions from the HSA are also tax when they are used for medical expenses.

The interest you pay on home mortgages and points paid at closing are tax deductible if you . So is the interest you pay on student loans when you itemize.

DEDUCTIONS THAT SAVE ON YOUR TAXES

Consider bundling medical deductions into certain tax years. You can only deduct medical expenses which exceed % of your 2024 AGI. If you already had some significant healthcare expenses for the year, see if you can move medical/dental expenses that you'd normally take early next year to the of this one.

Long-term Care Insurance premiums for LTC insurance are deductible with the amount of the deduction determined by your age. These deductions in 2025 can range from:

- $1,800 for those 50-60
- $4,810 for those 60-70
- $6,020 if you are over 70

TAX SAVINGS THROUGH CHARITABLE CONTRIBUTIONS

Kathleen Coxwell writes, "Charitable contributions of up to 60% of your AGI are also deductible if you and give to a qualified charity. Instead of making annual charitable gifts, give 2,3,4 or even 5 years' worth of donations in a year, then take a few years off." You can carry forward cash charitable giving above annual deduction limits for up to 5 years.

- Normally, you can deduct up to 60% of your AGI of cash donations.
- Appreciated securities are limited to 30% of AGI.

DONOR-ADVISED FUND (DAF)

A Donor-Advised Fund may be an option if you are bundling charitable expenses. A DAF is a private fund administered by a third party and created for the purpose of charitable donations on behalf of an organization, family, or individual. Per Fidelity, "A DAF may allow for tax-deductible contributions of cash or appreciated assets in a given year, but then control the timing of the to charity in future years."

Jessica McBride writes, "Gift appreciated securities, such as mutual funds, ETFs, or individual stocks to minimize future capital gains." While Taylor Turner writes, "You won't owe capital gains tax on the donated asset, you'll still receive a charitable donation, and you'll meet your goals—possibly having paid less out of pocket.

QUALIFIED CHARITABLE DISTRIBUTION (QCD)

Donate up to $100,000 annually from your IRA to a qualified charity through a Qualified Charitable Distribution. (As long as you're at least 73 when making the gift, and the check is payable directly to the qualified charity—then the shouldn't be taxable income, but should satisfy at least a portion of your Required Minimum Distribution (RMD).)

LEAVE A BEQUEST TO CHARITY

Taylor Turner writes, "Naming a charity as a beneficiary or leaving a bequest in your will or allows you to give to causes that are meaningful to you without overextending yourself. You don't want to run out of money in retirement due to of life, or the need to spend more on long-term care in your future."

RETIRING EARLY? KNOW YOUR WITHDRAWAL OPTIONS

Kathleen Coxwell outlines legal provisions in the tax laws that allow early withdrawal from tax advantaged accounts without penalty. She writes, "Traditional retirement savings vehicles like 401(k)s and IRAs enforce a % early withdrawal penalty made before age 59 ½. However, there are a couple of ways around the rules. You may want to more about the 72(t) and Rule of 55 provisions— ways to make penalty-free withdrawals from your retirement accounts BEFORE you turn 59 ½.

EARLY WITHDRAWAL OF RETIREMENT FUNDS IS NOT RECOMMENDED

Kathleen Coxwell writes, "The downsides to penalty-free withdrawal include:

1. No penalty, but you do need to pay applicable taxes.
2. If the money is spent, it is no longer growing. You not only want to think about the money you are spending, but also the potential growth on the money that you are losing.
3. You increase your risk of running out of money in retirement.
4. The withdrawal strategies are complicated and you don't want to get them wrong and end up paying the 10% penalty."

WHAT ORDER SHOULD YOU WITHDRAW FUNDS FOR RETIREMENT?

Kathleen Coxwell writes, "Conventional wisdom holds that you should by drawing on the taxable account assets, and then next move to the tax accounts, saving the Roth accounts, which are tax-free, for last or for passing on as a legacy. However, you want to remain flexible. It may not necessarily be advantageous to strictly follow the guidelines, and it is in fact ideal to keep assets in each type of account to be able to tap into them throughout your lifetime. This allows for added flexibility to both help lower your overall tax and also spread taxes out over time so you don't have to pay them all at once.

Patrick Villanova recently reported that a Fidelity study found that you can reduce your retirement lifetime total tax bill by taking a percentage withdrawal from all types of retirement accounts.

If you are in a low tax bracket, taking capital gains from your investments may be a good idea. Consider if now may be a good time to sell stocks that have appreciated significantly in value. This can be a particularly good if you are in the 10% or 12% Federal Tax brackets, since your capital gains tax may be zero.

STRATEGIZE FOR ROTH IRA CONVERSIONS

Kathleen Coxwell writes, "You can pay taxes , but avoid paying taxes on your gains if you save in a Roth IRA account. (Roth IRAs do not have Required Minimum Distributions (RMDs), although Roth 401(k)s do.) Should you do a Roth IRA conversion from your IRA? Knowing when to do a conversion can be confusing. Consider a Roth conversion if these situations apply, and you have the on hand to pay the taxes:

1. You anticipate a higher future tax rate.
2. You are hoping to leave money to heirs.
3. You expect future returns to be higher because the market has fallen. If you do a Roth conversion before you see those big gains then you will be paying taxes on a lower dollar amount and all growth will be tax free.
4. Withdrawals are a long way off.
5. You don't need the money from RMDs.
6. You anticipate an income in the future above the allowable for contributions.
7. The rate of return you anticipate making on the Roth IRA funds.
8. The amount of money in Traditional IRAs and the value of RMD when you are (73)."

TAX LOSS HARVESTING

Tax loss harvesting allows you to get rid of your investments while profiting a little from the transaction. You are only taxed on net capital gains—the amount you gained minus any investment —so any realized losses can help lower your tax bill. Therefore, if you know you're going to have realized gains, it may make sense to look for opportunities to realize losses to them...

If you have shares of funds or stocks that have lost value since you purchased them, you may want to consider selling them. In fact, if you have more losses than gains, you can use the extra losses to [illegible] up to $3,000 of ordinary taxable income (including the RMDs from your Traditional IRAs) on your Federal Income Taxes. You can also "carry forward" losses to future tax years. Be aware of the "[illegible] sale rule" which says you can't buy a similar fund or security within 30 days before or after a tax loss harvest.

CONCLUSION

Tax planning should be a big part of your retirement plan. Forethought can help you retain much more of your hard earned money. Consult with your CPA or CFP to help implement the best tax saving strategies for your unique situation. A stock index mutual fund is the wisest choice for taxable accounts as it is very tax efficient. Keep actively managed stock mutual funds, bonds, high dividend paying stocks, REITs, and junk bond funds in tax sheltered accounts. Always max out your tax sheltered savings prior to placing investments in taxable accounts. Buy and hold your stock mutual fund investments for at least one year to avoid short-term capital gains taxes. Use all legal tax deductions and credits on your taxes!

ACTION STEPS

1. Have you been considering the tax consequences of your investment portfolio?

   Exam how you have distributed assets between taxable and tax sheltered accounts. Use only tax sheltered accounts for your investments until you have maxed out your contributions to these accounts.

2. If you have taxable investment accounts are you using tax efficient index funds in these accounts?

   If not, consider making a change to tax efficient low cost index funds.

3. Are you using Roth IRA contributions to decrease any tax consequences of leaving a legacy to your children, and/or to lower your taxes in retirement?

   If you have a long time horizon, and/or are in a lower income tax bracket this may be an ideal time to invest in a Roth IRA.

LESSON 17

ESTATE PLANNING

"What will you do in the day of reckoning?...Where will you leave your riches."
ISAIAH 10:3

"I have seen...wealth hoarded to the harm of its owners, or wealth lost through misfortune, so that when they have children there is nothing left to inherit. Everyone comes naked from their mother's womb , and as everyone comes, so they depart. They take nothing from their toil that they can carry in their hands. As everyone comes, so they depart."
ECCLESIASTES 5:13-15

"So David made extensive preparations before his death."
1 CHRONICLES 22:5

WHY HAVE AN ESTATE PLAN?

Cheryl Kirsten writes, "A smart estate plan lets you stay in control. Without a plan in place, you don't get to ____________ who gets everything you've worked for your whole life."

"Moreover, no one knows when their ____________ will come." ECCLESIASTES 9:12

"Everyone is but a breath, even those who seem secure...In vain they rush about, heaping up wealth without ____________ whose it will finally be." PSALM 39:5-6

"If you want to be the one making those decisions, then you need an ____________ plan. And when there are so many factors outside of your control, it's important to spend time planning for the things ______ can control." Stacy Johnson and Miranda Marquit write, "The reality today is that 45% of people over 55 years old don't even have a will."

"This is what the LORD says, 'Put your ____________ in order, because you are going to die.'" ISAIAH 38:1
2 KINGS 20:1

"Teach us to ____________ our days, that we may gain a heart of wisdom." PSALM 90:12

WHAT IS ESTATE PLANNING?

"Estate planning is the process of creating ____________ documents to specify how and by whom your assets will be handled in the event of your ____________ or if you are unable to make decisions for yourself."

"An estate plan involves having a will, setting up a ________, selecting beneficiaries for retirement accounts, and life insurance policies, and how you ________ ownership of assets including your home."

"Be careful not to ________ this matter." EZRA 4:22

"Do not be overawed when others grow rich, when the splendor of their houses increases; for they will take ________ with them when they die." PSALM 49:16-17

LAST WILL AND TESTAMENT

"A will is a set of instructions explaining how property owned in your name should be ________ after your passing. It also names the Executor of your estate, and a Guardian for minors if needed." When choosing an Executor, you want to ask somebody who is ________ oriented, maybe somebody in your family who's a lawyer, accountant, or somebody really trustworthy. It wouldn't be a bad idea to name a ________ Executor, in the case of the onset of dementia or the death of your first executor choice.

"In the case of a will, it is necessary to prove the ________ of the one who made it, because a will is in force only when somebody has died; it never takes effect while the one who made it is living." HEBREWS 9:16-17

Marilyn Lewis writes, "A will gives you the power to ________ what is in the best interests of your children and pets after you are gone, and designate any assets you are leaving for their care. It also can help you determine what will happen to possessions with ________ or sentimental value."

"In the absence of a trust your will is sent to ________ court, and these proceedings become a matter of public record, with the ability of individuals to ________ the validity of these instructions in light of any other relevant information. It is important to keep private information, such as ________, out of your will, as that information could become a matter of public record."

THE REVOCABLE LIVING TRUST

The Revocable Living Trust is "one often ________ estate planning tool…Trusts offer more control and ________ than wills, and they can help make your estate plan more flexible." A trust passes assets to heirs while avoiding potentially expensive and ________ consuming probate court. You name a Trustee, perhaps your spouse, family member or attorney to manage your property. Unlike a will, a trust can be used to distribute ________ now or after your death. You should find a qualified estate attorney to help you create a Revocable Living Trust.

DURABLE POWER OF ATTORNEY

"It will be important to have Power of Attorneys in place. A Power of Attorney (POA) is a person you designate to manage your ________ when you are no longer able to do so. Don't put off choosing someone, because you must be legally competent to assign this role. There are two types of POAs you need to designate. The first is a Financial and Legal POA who manages decisions surrounding your finances. A second POA is a Health Care Power of Attorney who is designated to handle decisions regarding your [illegible] care in the event you become incapacitated. "One of the most sensitive topics to discuss…is what will happen if you become [illegible] to manage your own estate, whether temporarily or permanently. It's important to have a plan in place so your financial and medical wishes are carried out."

A LIVING WILL

"A Living Will and Advanced Medical Directive outline what your preferences are concerning medical treatment in [illegible] situations…A Living Will details instructions concerning end-of-life care only." A Living Will allows you to explain in advance of terminal illness what types of care you do and [illegible] want in case you can't communicate that in the future. It is strictly a place to spell out your health [illegible] preferences. You can say as much or as little as you wish about the kind of health care you want to receive in your Living Will.

DESIGNATE BENEFICIARIES

Make sure to review your beneficiary information on all [illegible] plans and insurance policies. "Beneficiary designations are important! Did you know you need to designate your IRA beneficiaries as 'per capita' or 'per stirpes'? Getting it right can make a big difference in how your wealth is transferred and whether it's [illegible] down the way you intend." "With a per capita designation, assets are divided equally among surviving co-beneficiaries, which means nothing will pass on to a deceased beneficiary's heirs. With a stirpes designation, if one of your beneficiaries is deceased, [illegible] portion will go to their surviving children."

"This is what the Sovereign LORD says; If the prince makes a gift from his inheritance to one of his sons, it will also [illegible] to his descendants; it is to be their property by inheritance." EZEKIEL 46:16

Make sure to "remember to update your beneficiaries as needed after big life events such as births or marriages." "These beneficiary designations take [illegible] over instructions in a will."

PROPER TITLING OF ASSETS

It is important to review that any assets [illegible] owned with your spouse are properly titled, the way you want, because how assets are titled may take precedence over [illegible] in your will.

DIGITAL ASSET TRUST

Marilyn Lewis writes, "You can use a Digital Asset Trust to decide what to do with your electronic property, including your hard drive, digital photos, cloud storage and [illegible] accounts such as Facebook… and Google. It is wise to create a separate list of your passwords."

LETTER OF INTENT

"The Letter of Intent is an opportunity to write instructions, requests and important personal or financial information that don't in your will. This may be a good place to give any detailed instructions about how you want your or memorial service to be performed. An attorney is not needed as this letter won't carry the weight of a will."

REVIEW ESTATE PLANS REGULARLY

"An estate plan isn't something you can set and forget…You want to make sure that your intentions haven't and you've included the right people. If it's been 5 years or more, it's time to review your estate plan to see if any updates are warranted. You may also want to check whether there have been any changes to the laws that could affect your plan. If you or your family have experienced any major life event, it's worth revisiting your plan."

PROTECT YOUR ESTATE FROM TAXES

Cheryl Kirsten writes, "Another benefit of a Revocable Living Trust is if you have substantial assets or wealth, a trust can be a way of tax savings." "When tax laws change it is important to review your portfolio to see how it might be …Armed with an effective tax strategy, you can avoid making mistakes that could eat into your estate. Planning for state estate taxes and any federal and state inheritance taxes is an important of estate planning."

MINIMIZING INHERITANCE TAXES

Cheryl Kirsten writes, "You can minimize inheritance taxes by giving money or property to family members or others your lifetime. You can:

1. Make annual gifts of up to $16,000 each per gift recipient, or $32,000 by a married couple.
2. Give an unlimited amount to charity.
3. Contribute to a loved one's 529 Educational Savings Plan…You can make up to 5 years of contributions at one time without incurring a federal gift tax.
4. Pay any amount toward another person's tuition or medical bills. You must pay the tuition directly to an institution on behalf of a loved one, and qualified medical payments must be made directly to the provider.
5. Invest in a Roth IRA…the primary benefit of a Roth IRA is that you pay taxes now so your beneficiaries won't have to pay them when they inherit your Roth IRA."

LEGACY PLANNING

Erin McClain writes, "Once you have an estate plan that captures where your assets will go upon your death and who can make financial and health care decisions if you become unable to do so, it's time to start thinking about legacy planning. This is where you'll shift your focus from finalizing legal documents to your family to inherit your wealth and execute your wishes."

"Consider this question: 'How prepared are your loved ones to inherit your wealth if something unexpected were to tomorrow?' This simple question reinforces the importance of legacy planning. The reasons families don't succeed in transferring their wealth are:

- 60% is lack of communication
- 25% is inadequate preparation
- 15% are other reasons such as lack of mission, taxes, legal, etc.

"For riches do not endure forever, and…is not for all generations." PROVERBS 27:24

"The key (to successful wealth transfer) starts with communication about your financial intentions. Your family should know what to expect when you pass away, including how they can best protect your and carry out your financial legacy."

"To this day their children and grandchildren to do as their ancestors did." 2 KINGS 17:41

"If you haven't already, set aside time with your partner…to get on the same page with long-term goals, and ensure you're both prepared if life brings any situations your way. Once your kids become young adults, bring them up to speed on your family's long-term wealth plan. Scheduling meetings at least a year is a good place to start." "Legacy meetings go a long way in creating around your decisions."

Educate your loved ones…to alleviate a sudden financial should something unexpected happen to the family financial lead. This can be done by involving your spouse in with any and all of your financial team including your Certified Financial Planner (CFP), Certified Public Accountant (CPA), and your Estate Planning Attorney. "Knowing that they have trusted professionals they can turn to can be extremely comforting if they're not to take on the responsibility alone." Along with that, "teaching them the basic financial concepts and investing they'll need to carry out your legacy will prepare them for the responsibilities that lie ahead."

LIST OF IMPORTANT DOCUMENTS

"Make sure your family knows where to find everything you've prepared. Be sure to keep a secure, easily accessible of your accounts and include the contact details for any financial associates you consult with including financial advisors, tax planners, estate planners, trustees, etc. Make a list of documents, including where is stored. Include papers for:

1. Bank Accounts: Make Bank Accounts Payable on Death to a beneficiary
2. List of Bills and Accounts: Include contact information and Account #s
3. Life Insurance Policies
4. Real Estate Deeds
5. Pension and Retirement Accounts

6. Stocks, Bonds, Mutual Funds, ETFs
7. Annuities
8. Birth and Adoption Certificates
9. Divorce Record

"Consolidating your assets and capturing the priority of financial decisions can help to the process" of resolving your estate in an efficient manner, and be much appreciated by those who survive your passing.

CONCLUSION

An estate plan allows you to choose who gets everything you've worked for your whole life. An estate plan involves having a will, setting up a trust, selecting beneficiaries for retirement accounts and life insurance policies, and how to title ownership of assets including your home. A Will is a set of instructions explaining how property owned in your name should be distributed after your passing. It also names the Executor of your estate, and a Guardian for minors. You need to name a Power of Attorney for your legal and financial decisions, as well as a Healthcare Power of Attorney. In the absence of a trust your Will is sent to probate court, and these proceedings become a matter of public record. To avoid probate court, and the public record, establish a Revocable Living Trust. A trust passes to heirs while avoiding potentially expensive and time consuming probate court. A Living Will is an advanced medical directive that outlines your preferences of medical care in an end of life situation or if you are unable to communicate.

ACTION STEPS

1. Do you have a Will or Revocable Living Trust?

If not, make it a priority in the next 3-6 months to get a Will or Revocable Living Trust completed. Your heirs will greatly appreciate your diligence in this matter.

2. Have you considered a Legacy Plan for preparing your heirs for receiving and investing their inheritance?

If your heirs are young adults it is time to start preparing them, first by educating them in financial planning and your legacy goals.

LESSON 18

GENEROUS GIVING

"Give, and it will be given to you. A good measure, pressed down, shaken together and running over, will be poured into your lap. For with the measure you use, it will be measured to you."

LUKE 6:38

*"Remember this: Whoever sows sparingly will also reap sparingly,
And whoever sows generously will also reap generously."*

2 CORINTHIANS 9:6

*"From everyone who has been given much, much will be demanded;
and from the one who has been entrusted with much, much more will be asked."*

LUKE 12:48

SHARING OUR BLESSINGS

When it comes to sharing our blessings, we must return to the principles of stewardship, that all things on earth __________ to God, and we're created by God, and God gives us the responsibility to care for and use the blessings He has provided us to __________ others.

"And God is able to bless you abundantly, so that in ______ things at all times, having all that you ________, you will abound in every good work." 2 CORINTHIANS 9:8

"If you spend yourselves in behalf of the hungry and ________ the needs of the oppressed, then your light will rise in the darkness, and your night will become like the noonday. The LORD will guide you always, He will __________ your needs in a sun-scorched land and will strengthen your frame. You will be a well-watered garden like a spring whose waters ______ fail." ISAIAH 58:10-11

LOVE YOUR NEIGHBOR AS YOURSELF

We are to love the LORD our God with all our heart, soul, mind and strength, and in the words of Leviticus 19:18 to: "Love our neighbor as yourself."

Although there is nothing ________ with becoming wealthy and financially (in)dependent, God has blessed us, so that we can bless others.

"Do not store up for yourselves treasures on earth...But store up for yourselves __________ in heaven." MATTHEW 6:19-20

"Do nothing out of selfish ambition or vain conceit. Rather, in humility value ______ above yourselves, not looking to ______ own interests but each of you to the interests of the other." **PHILIPPIANS 2:2-4**

EXCEL IN THE GRACE OF GIVING

As mature Christians giving should become natural, a fruit of the Spirit.

"But since you excel in everything—in faith, in speech, in knowledge, in complete earnestness and in love we have kindled in you—see that you also excel in this ______ of giving." **CORINTHIANS 8:7**

"Freely you have received; ______ give." **MATTHEW 10:8**

It is God who works through your generosity to fulfill His purposes.

"For it is God who works in you to will and to ______ in order to fulfill His good purpose." **PHILIPPIANS 2:13**

A GENEROUS PERSON WILL PROSPER

When it comes to giving, Jesus' own words are given to us:

"Remembering the words of the Lord Jesus Himself said: 'It is more blessed to ______ than to receive.'" **ACTS 20:35**

Many times the person who gives generously, receives blessings equal to or greater than the gifts they offer!

"One person gives freely, yet gains even ______ ; another ______ unduly, but comes to poverty." **PROVERBS 11:24**

"A generous person will prosper; whoever ______ others will be refreshed." **PROVERBS 11:25**

"Give to them as the LORD your God has ______ you." **DEUTERONOMY 15:14**

"As water reflects the face, so one's ______ reflects the heart." **PROVERBS 27:19**

DON'T PUT YOUR HOPE IN WEALTH

Paul gives those who are rich this command:

"Command those who are rich in this present world not to be arrogant nor to put their ______ in wealth, which is so uncertain, but to put their hope in ______ ...Command them to do good, to be rich in good deeds, and to be ______ and willing to share. In this way they will lay up treasure for themselves as a firm foundation for the coming age, so that they may take hold of the life that is truly life (eternal life)." **1 TIMOTHY 6:17-19**

LOVE LIKE JESUS

"This is how love is made ____________ among us...In this world we are like Jesus." 1 JOHN 4:17

"But if we love one another, God lives in us and His ____________ is made complete in us." 1 JOHN 4:12

So we are to be like Jesus in our daily lives, through the Holy Spirit moving into action to do good works.

"Dear children, let us not love with words or speech but with ____________ and in truth." 1 JOHN 3:18

"For we are God's handiwork, created in Christ Jesus to do good works, which God prepared in ____________ for us to do." EPHESIANS 2:10

ACT IN LOVE BY DOING GOOD

This theme of doing good is a thread throughout Scriptures.

"For in Christ Jesus...the only thing that counts is faith ____________ itself through love." GALATIANS 5:6

"Brothers and sisters, never ____________ of doing what is good." 2 THESSALONIANS 3:13

And we can be assured that Christ is with us as we endeavor to do good.

"God...by His power He may bring to fruition your every ____________ for goodness and your every ____________ prompted by faith." 2 THESSALONIANS 1:11

"Our people must learn to ____________ themselves to doing what is good, in order to provide for ____________ needs, and not live unproductive lives." TITUS 3:14

"And I want to stress these things, so that those who have trusted in God may be careful to devote themselves in ____________ what is good. These things are excellent and profitable for everyone." TITUS 3:8

ESPECIALLY BLESS OUR FELLOW CHRISTIANS

We should be especially concerned for our brothers and sisters in Christ.

"Therefore as we have opportunity, let us do good to all people, especially to those who belong to the ____________ of believers." GALATIANS 6:10

And we should not tire of doing good as God will bless our efforts in His timing.

"Let us not become ____________ in doing good, for at the proper time we will reap a harvest if we do not give up." GALATIANS 6:9

"Do not withhold good from those to whom it is due, when it is in your ____________ to act." PROVERBS 3:27

"Faith by itself, if not accompanied by action, is ______." JAMES 2:17

"You see that his faith and his actions were working ______, and his faith was made complete by what he did." JAMES 2:22

"Being confident of this, that He who began a good work in you will carry it on to ______ until the day of Christ Jesus." PHILIPPIANS 1:6

GOD IS PLEASED WITH OUR ACTIONS FOR GOOD

Your actions of doing good will be recognized by God and man.

"Let love and faithfulness never leave you…Then you will win favor with a good name in the ______ of God and man." PROVERBS 3:3-4

"God is not unjust; He will not ______ your work and the love you have shown as you have helped God's people and continue to help them." HEBREWS 6:10

"And do not forget to do good and to ______ with others, for with such sacrifices God is pleased." HEBREWS 13:16

CARING FOR THE POOR

Jesus considers our work to help the poor something you have done for Him, as His hands and feet to the world.

"For I was hungry and you gave Me something to eat, I was thirsty and you gave Me something to drink, I was a stranger and you invited Me in, I needed clothes and you clothed Me, I was sick and you looked after Me, I was in prison and you came to visit Me…Truly I tell you, whatever you did for one of the ______ of these brothers of mine, you did for Me." MATTHEW 25:35-36 AND 40

"Whoever oppresses the poor shows contempt for their Maker, but whoever is kind to the ______ honors God." PROVERBS 14:31

CARING FOR THE POOR LEADS TO BLESSINGS

"The generous will themselves be ______, for they share their food with the poor." PROVERBS 22:9

"They have ______ scattered their ______ to the poor; their righteousness endures forever." PSALM 112:9 / 2 CORINTHIANS 9:9

"Whoever is kind to the poor lends to the LORD, and He will ______ them for what they have done." PROVERBS 19:17

"Blessed is the one who is ______ to the needy." PROVERBS 14:21

"Those who ______ to the poor will lack ______, but those who close their eyes to them receive many curses." PROVERBS 28:27

WE ARE BLESSED WHEN GIVING WITH OPEN-HANDS

"Give generously to them (the needy among you) and do so without a grudging heart; then because of this the LORD your God will bless you in ______ your work and in everything you put your hand to. There will always be poor people in the land. Therefore I command you to be ______ - ______ toward fellow Israelites (citizens) who are poor and needy in your land." DEUTERONOMY 15:10-11

"She opens her arms to the poor and extends her ______ to the needy." PROVERBS 31:20

"If anyone is poor among...you, do not be hardhearted or ______ toward them. Rather, be open-handed and freely lend them whatever they need." DEUTERONOMY 15:7-8

BEING GENEROUS OPENS GOD'S EAR TO YOUR PRAYERS

Being generous opens the lines of communication through prayer with God.

"Cornelius, God has heard your ______ and remembered your gifts to the poor." ACTS 10:31

As you are generous to others, you may be able to insert your name for that of Cornelius, and God may answer your prayers.

"Is it not this kind of fasting I have chosen: to loose the chains of injustice and untie the cords of the yoke, to set the oppressed free and break every yoke. Is it not to ______ your food with the hungry and to provide the poor wanderer with shelter—when you see the naked, to clothe them, and not turn away from your own flesh and blood? Then your light will break forth like the dawn, and healing will quickly appear; then your ______ will go before you, and the glory of the LORD will be your ______ guard. Then you will call, and the LORD will ______, you will cry for help, and I will say: Hear am I." ISAIAH 58:6-9

THE POOR HAVE A GREATER GIFT IN CHRIST

It is better to be a faithful follower of Jesus Christ and be poor, than to be rich and not gain the eternal blessing given through faith in Christ.

"Better the poor whose walk is ______ than the rich whose ways are perverse." PROVERBS 28:6

"Religion that God our Father accepts as pure and faultless is this: to look after orphans and widows in their distress and to ______ oneself from being polluted by the world." JAMES 1:27

"Better a little with   than much gain with injustice." **PROVERBS 16:8**

"Listen, my dear brothers and sisters: Has not God chosen those who are poor in the eyes of the world to be   in faith and to inherit the kingdom He promised those who love Him?" **JAMES 2:5**

"I know your afflictions and your   —yet you are rich!" **REVELATION 2:9**

Rich in faith, and knowledge of Jesus Christ their Savior.

IF YOUR SPIRITUAL GIFT IS GIVING—GIVE GENEROUSLY

"We have different gifts, according to the grace given to each of us. If your gift is…giving, then   generously." **ROMANS 12:6 & 8**

"Each of you should use whatever gift you have received to   others, as faithful stewards of God's grace in its various forms." **1 PETER 4:10**

When we give with a joyful heart we can be sure our giving aligns with God's mission. Paul points out what a great Christian example the people of the Macedonian church were when they acted in faith:

"In the midst of a very severe trial, their overflowing joy and their extreme poverty welled up in   generosity. For I testify that they gave as much as they were   , and even beyond their ability." **2 CORINTHIANS 8:2-3**

GOD HAS A HEART FOR THE WEARY, WEAK AND POOR

"I know that the LORD secures justice for the   and upholds the cause of the needy." **PSALM 140:12**

When something is consistent with God's character, it should also be consistent with our character.

"'He defended the cause of the poor and needy, and so all went well. Is that not what it means to   me?' declares the LORD." **JEREMIAH 22:16**

The Bible points out how God meets the needs of the weary, weak, poor and marginalized in society.

"Though the LORD is exalted, He looks   on the lowly." **PSALM 138:6**

"He upholds the cause of the oppressed and gives   to the hungry." **PSALM 146:7**

"The LORD does   let the righteous go hungry." **PROVERBS 10:3**

"But He   the needy out of their affliction." **PSALM 107:41**

"He raises the poor from the dust and lifts the   from the ash heap." **PSALM 113:7**

GOD DESIRES OUR GENEROSITY TO GIVE GLORY TO HIM

"You will be enriched in every way so that you can be on every occasion, and through us your generosity will result in to God. This service that you perform is not only supplying the needs of the Lord's people but is also overflowing in many expressions of to God. Because of the service by which you proved yourselves, others will praise God for the obedience that accompanies your confession of the gospel of Christ, and for your generosity in with them and with everyone else." 2 CORINTHIANS 9:11-13

CONCLUSION

God has blessed us so that we can bless others. As mature Christians giving should be a natural fruit of the Spirit. God works through your generosity to fulfill His purposes. Many times the person who gives, receives blessings equal to or greater than the gifts they offer. As maturing Christians we are to be like Jesus. It is our faith and actions working together that pleases God. Jesus considers our work to help the poor something you have done for Him, as His hands and feet to the world. We are to be open-handed to those we find in need. If your spiritual gift is giving—give generously!

ACTION STEPS

1. Have you recently blessed others through your God given blessings?

Try to find a way of blessing others this week with your blessings. Maybe you can do the "drive thru difference," and pay for the meals for the car behind you.

2. What have you recently done for the poor?

If it has been a while, try volunteering at a food shelf, or an organization like Feed My Starving Children. After serving, give to purchase meals for those in need.

LESSON 19

CONCLUSIONS

"How great is God—-beyond our understanding!"
JOB 36:26

"But wisdom is shown to be right by the lives of those who follow it."
LUKE 7:35 NLT

"Submit to God and be at peace with Him; In this way prosperity will come to you."
JOB 22:21

"WHAT WILL THE OUTCOME OF ALL THIS BE?"
DANIEL 12:8

We've covered a lot of territory when it comes to God honoring personal financial health. Do not become overwhelmed by all the information. I intentionally included some information that was new to me, and might at some point become useful to you.

"My words come from an upright heart; my lips sincerely speak what I know." JOB 33:3

Take your personal goal of financial (in)dependence on God as a journey to be completed one step at a time.

"You know that I have not hesitated to preach anything that would be helpful to you...For I have not hesitated to proclaim to you the whole will of God." ACTS 20:20 & 27

"I have spoken to you with great frankness." 2 CORINTHIANS 7:4

FINANCIAL (IN)DEPENDENCE

The whole concept of Financial (In)dependence is based on the truth that all our financial blessings come from God and Him alone. We are dependent on Him!

"But their prosperity is not in their own hands." JOB 21:16

We must pay attention to how God is guiding us.

"I, the LORD, speak the truth: I declare what is right." ISAIAH 45:19

"Whether you turn to the right or to the left, your ears will hear a voice behind you, saying, 'This is the way; walk in it.'" ISAIAH 30:21

I would like you to join me on this journey:

"Join together in following my example, brothers and sisters, and just as you have us as a model, keep your eyes on those who live as we do." PHILIPPIANS 3:17

"What I am saying is true and reasonable." ACTS 26:25

"We have examined this, and it is true. So hear it and apply it to yourself." JOB 5:27

WILL YOU TRUST GOD AT HIS EVERY PROMISE AND RECEIVE THE BLESSINGS HE DESIRES FOR YOU?

"You know with all your heart and soul that not one of all the good promises the LORD your God gave you has failed. EVERY PROMISE HAS BEEN FULFILLED; not one has failed." JOSHUA 23:14

"Be sure to fear the LORD and serve Him faithfully with all your heart, consider what great things He has done for you." 1 SAMUEL 12:24

"For no word from God will ever fail." LUKE 1:37

WILL YOU EXAMINE GOD'S CHARACTER AND, WITH THE POWER OF THE HOLY SPIRIT, MORE FAITHFULLY SIMULATE IT AS A DISCIPLE OF JESUS? AS SOMEONE WHO DESIRES THE FINANCIAL BLESSINGS GOD DESIRES TO PROVIDE, WILL YOU EMULATE THE POSITIVE CHARACTERISTICS OF THE WEALTHY INCLUDING THE SELF-DISCIPLINE NECESSARY TO BECOME FINANCIALLY (IN)DEPENDENT?

"He has shown you, O mortal, what is good. And what does the LORD require of you? To act justly and to love mercy and to walk humbly with your God." MICAH 6:8

"Make every effort to add to your faith goodness; and to goodness, knowledge; and to knowledge, self-control; and to self-control, perseverance; and to perseverance, godliness; and to godliness; mutual affection; and to mutual affection, love. For if you possess these qualities in increasing measure, they will keep you from being ineffective and unproductive in your knowledge of our LORD Jesus Christ." 2 PETER 1:5-8

WILL YOU FIND GOD HONORING WORK THAT USES THE GIFTS HE HAS GIVEN, TO SUPPORT YOUR FAMILY AND GOD'S MISSION ON EARTH?

"All hard work brings a profit, but mere talk leads only to poverty? PROVERBS 14:23

"A man can do nothing better than to eat and drink and find satisfaction in his work. This too, I see, is from the hand of God." ECCLESIASTES 2:24

"So I commend the enjoyment of life, because there is nothing better for a person under the sun than to eat and drink and be glad. Then joy will accompany them in their toil (work) and the days of the life God has given them under the sun." ECCLESIASTES 8:15

WILL YOU TITHE (GIVE AT LEAST 10%) TO YOUR LOCAL CHRISTIAN CHURCH AS A WAY OF RETURNING TO GOD, A PORTION OF HIS BLESSINGS TO YOU?

"On the first day of the week, each one of you should set aside a sum of money in keeping with your income, saving it up." 1 CORINTHIANS 16:2

"Each of you should give what you have decided in your heart to give, not reluctantly or under compulsion, for God loves a cheerful giver." 2 CORINTHIANS 9:7

WILL YOU DO A ZERO BASED BUDGET TO RECONCILE THE MONEY YOU HAVE COMING IN AS SALARY WITH MONEY YOU SPEND ON A MONTHLY BASIS?

"Be sure to know the condition of your flocks, give careful attention to your herds (finances); for riches do not endure forever." PROVERBS 27:23-24

"Be very careful, then, how you live—not as unwise but as wise." EPHESIANS 5:15

"Whoever loves discipline loves knowledge." PROVERBS 12:1

WILL YOU BE A FAITHFUL STEWARD OF GOD'S GIFTS, AND COMPLETE A DEBT REDUCTION PLAN UNTIL ALL DEBT BESIDES YOUR MORTGAGE IS ELIMINATED?

"What is mankind that You are mindful of them, human beings that You care for them: You made them rulers over the works of Your hands; You put everything under their feet." PSALM 8:4-6

"Do not conform to the pattern of this world, but be transformed by the renewing of your mind. Then you will be able to test and approve what God's will is, His good, pleasing and perfect will." ROMANS 12:2

"No discipline seems pleasant at the time, but painful. Later on, however, it produces a harvest of righteousness and peace for those who have been trained by it." HEBREWS 12:11

WILL YOU PROVIDE SOME MARGIN FOR YOUR FAMILY AND YOUR LIFE BY SAVING FOR A 3-9 MONTH EMERGENCY FUND?

"Disaster will come upon you, and you will not know how to conjure it away. A calamity will fall upon you that you cannot ward off with a ransom; a catastrophe you cannot foresee will suddenly come upon you." ISAIAH 47:11

"So that no one would be unsettled by these trials. For you know quite well that we are destined for them." 1 THESSALONIANS 3:3

"Have you entered the storehouses...which I reserved for times of trouble." JOB 38:22-23

WILL YOU APPLY THE INVESTING PRINCIPLES OF USING LOW COST INDEX MUTUAL FUNDS, DOLLAR-COST-AVERAGING, AND INVESTING A MINIMUM OF 15% TOWARDS YOUR RETIREMENT?

"Many, LORD, are asking, 'Who will bring us prosperity?' Let the light of Your face shine on us." PSALM 4:6

"But remember the LORD your God, for it is He who gives you the ability to produce wealth." DEUTERONOMY 8:18

"What you heard from me, keep as the pattern of sound teaching, with faith and love in Christ Jesus." 2 TIMOTHY 1:13

WILL YOU AVOID SELLING STOCKS (OR STOCK MUTUAL FUNDS) IN A DECLINING STOCK ENVIRONMENT BY AVOIDING FEAR THROUGH TRUSTING GOD AT HIS WORD AND DOLLAR-COST-AVERAGE THROUGH STOCK MARKET DEPRESSIONS?

"I have seen something else under the sun: The race is not to the swift or the battle to the strong, nor does food come to the wise or wealth to the brilliant or favor to the learned; but time and chance happen to them all." ECCLESIASTES 9:11

"You will stand firm and without fear." JOB 11:15

"But wisdom is proved right by her deeds." MATTHEW 11:19

WILL YOU USE INDEX MUTUAL FUNDS TO DIVERSIFY YOUR STOCK, BOND, AND REIT PORTFOLIO, AND USE AN ASSET ALLOCATION THAT IS SPECIFIC TO YOUR PERSONAL RISK TOLERANCE AND INVESTMENT TIME HORIZON?

"But divide your investments among many places, for you do not know what risks might be ahead." ECCLESIASTES 11:2 NLT

"For you do not know which will succeed, whether this or that, or whether both will do equally well." ECCLESIASTES 11:6

"The Word of the LORD to them will become: Do this, do that, a rule for this, a rule for that, a little here, a little there." ISAIAH 28:13

WILL YOU WRITE A FAMILY FINANCIAL PLAN THAT MEETS YOUR FAMILY'S PERSONAL FINANCIAL AND INVESTING GOALS, AND EVALUATE YOUR PLAN YEARLY FOR ANY NEEDED CHANGES?

"Commit to the LORD whatever you do, and He will establish your plan." PROVERBS 16:3

"He will teach us His ways so that we may walk in His paths." ISAIAH 2:3 & MICAH 4:2

"There is no wisdom, no plan that can succeed against the LORD." PROVERBS 21:30

"As for God, His way is perfect:...The LORD's word is flawless; He shields all who take refuge in Him." 2 SAMUEL 22:31 & PSALM 18:10

WILL YOU EXAMINE YOUR PERSONAL FINANCE BEHAVIORAL BIASES AND MAKE A PLAN TO MITIGATE THEM?

"Reform your ways and actions." JEREMIAH 18:11

"Teach them His decrees and instructions, and show them the way they are to live and how they are to behave." EXODUS 18:20

"He set my feet on a rock and gave me a firm place to stand." PSALM 40:2

WILL YOU BE CAREFUL WITH THE FINANCIAL ASPECTS OF YOUR LARGEST FINANCIAL PURCHASE OF BUYING A HOME?

"Suppose one of you wants to build a tower (home). Won't you first sit down and estimate the cost to see if you have enough money to complete it? For if you lay the foundation and are not able to finish it, everyone who sees it will ridicule you, saying, 'This person began to build and wasn't able to finish.'" LUKE 14:28-30

"For every house is built by someone, but God is the builder of everything." HEBREWS 3:4

"My people will live in peaceful dwelling places, in secure homes, in undisturbed places of rest." ISAIAH 32:18

WILL YOU START INVESTING FOR RETIREMENT IN YOUR EARLY TWENTIES, AND CONTINUE TO INVEST 15% OF YOUR SALARY, OR MORE, USING CATCH UP CONTRIBUTIONS IF YOU STARTED INVESTING LATE, UNTIL YOU REACH FINANCIAL (IN)DEPENDENCE?

"I was young and now I am old, yet I have never seen the righteous forsaken or their children begging bread." PSALM 37:25

"I am very rich; I have become wealthy. With all my wealth they will not find in me any iniquity or sin." HOSEA 12:8

"Better one handful with tranquility than two handfuls with toil and chasing after the wind." ECCLESIASTES 4:6

"But godliness with contentment is great gain." 1 TIMOTHY 6:6

"Moreover, when God gives someone wealth and possessions, and the ability to enjoy them, to accept their lot and be happy in their toil—this is a gift of God. They seldom reflect on the days of their life, because God keeps them occupied with gladness of heart." ECCLESIASTES 5:19-20

WILL YOU DEFEND YOUR FINANCES FROM DISASTER AND PROTECT YOUR FAMILY BY PURCHASING APPROPRIATE INSURANCE?

"A catastrophe you cannot foresee will suddenly come upon you." ISAIAH 45:7

"Watch out that you do not lose what we have worked for, but that you may be rewarded fully." 2 JOHN 1:8

"Any man or woman who wrongs another in any way…must confess the sin they have committed. They must make full restitution for the wrong they have done." NUMBERS 5:6-7

WILL YOU PLAN YOUR INVESTING WISELY AND MINIMIZE TAXES BY USING TAX ADVANTAGE SAVINGS ACCOUNTS AND ANY OTHER LEGAL AND SPIRITUALLY ACCEPTABLE MEANS TO ONLY PAY YOUR FAIR SHARE?

"Then Jesus said to them, 'Give to Caesar what is Caesar's, and to God what is God's.'" MARK 12:17 MATTHEW 22:21 LUKE 20:25

"Give everyone what you owe him: If you owe taxes, pay taxes; if revenue, then revenue; if respect, then respect; if honor, then honor." ROMANS 13:7

"He taxed the land and exacted the silver and gold from the people of the land according to their assessment." 2 KINGS 23:35

WILL YOU WRITE A WILL AND/OR USE A REVOCABLE LIVING TRUST TO IMPROVE THE TRANSFER OF WEALTH TO YOUR HEIRS AND/OR YOUR CHURCH?

"So David made extensive preparations before his death." 1 CHRONICLES 22:5

"What will you do in the day of reckoning?...Where will you leave your riches?" ISAIAH 10:3

"I have seen…wealth hoarded to the harm of its owners, or wealth lost through misfortune, so that when they have children there is nothing left to inherit. Everyone comes naked from their mother's womb, and as everyone comes, so they depart. They take nothing from their toil that they can carry in their hands. As everyone comes, so they depart." ECCLESIASTES 5:13-15

WILL YOU BE THANKFUL FOR THE BLESSINGS GOD HAS PROVIDED FOR YOUR FAMILY, AND SHARE YOUR BLESSINGS WITH OTHERS BY GIVING GENEROUSLY?

"Wealth and honor come from You…Now, our God, we give You thanks, and praise Your glorious name." 1 CHRONICLES 29:12-13

"Give thanks in all circumstances; for this is God's will for you in Christ Jesus." 1 THESSALONIANS 5:18

"Command those who are rich in this present world not to be arrogant nor to put their hope in wealth, which is so uncertain, but to put their hope in God, who richly provides us with everything for our enjoyment. Command them to do good, to be rich in good deeds, and to be generous and willing to share. In this way they will lay up treasure for themselves as a firm foundation for the coming age, so that they may take hold of the life that is truly life (eternal life)." 1 TIMOTHY 6:17-19

WHY TRY TO GO THROUGH ALL THE ACTIONS AND SELF-DISCIPLINE REQUIRED TO REACH GOD HONORING FINANCIAL (IN)DEPENDENCE?

Plain and simply for the peace God provides as we trust in Him to provide for our every need.

"LORD, you establish peace for us; all that we have accomplished you have done for us." ISAIAH 26:12

We should aspire to receive just enough blessings from God so that we can maintain a strong personal relationship with Him.

"Give me neither poverty nor riches, but give me only my daily bread. Otherwise, I may have too much and disown you and say, 'Who is the LORD?' or I may become poor and steal, and so dishonor the name of my God." Proverbs 30:8-9

GOD HONORING FINANCIAL (IN)DEPENDENCE ON HIM

"This is what the LORD says: 'Let not the wise boast of their wisdom or the strong boast of their strength or the rich boast of their riches, but let the one who boasts boast about this: that they have the understanding to know Me, that I AM the LORD." JEREMIAH 9:23-24

"So then, brothers and sisters, stand firm and hold fast to the teachings we passed on to you, whether by word of mouth or by letter. May our Lord Jesus Christ himself and God our Father, who loved us and by grace gave us eternal encouragement and good hope, encourage your hearts and strengthen you in every good deed and word. 2 THESSALONIANS 2:15-17

THE TWENTY COMMANDMENTS OF GOD HONORING FINANCIAL (IN)DEPENDENCE

1. Be mindful and plan your spending. Live below your means.
2. Live off a budget so you know where your dollars are going.
3. Work as if working for the Lord in all that you do.
4. Return to the Lord the gifts that are His, a minimum of 10% of take home pay, and He promises to bless you by opening His storehouse.
5. Eliminate debt and save for large purchases.
6. Maintain a 3 to 9 month emergency fund, of budgeted spending, for covering unexpected expenses or a job loss.
7. Purchase insurance to avoid large financial losses: especially Term Life, Long Term Disability, Auto, Homeowners, Health, and Long Term Care.
8. Automate your savings and investing, so you don't even see the money.
9. Dollar-cost-average your investment dollars by investing a set amount (15% of pay) on a regular basis, no matter what the stock market is doing.
10. Keep your costs of investing low by using index mutual funds or ETFs as the foundation of your investment portfolio.
11. Begin investing at an early age to take advantage of the miracle of compound interest. The earlier you start the less you'll have to invest to reach financial (in)dependence. It is time in the market that creates successful investors.
12. Do not try to time the stock market, because you have to get two decisions right, when to get out, and when to get back in. Always stay fully invested at a stock allocation that allows good sleep.
13. Do not allow your emotions about money (a paper loss from a market downturn) guide your financial decision making.
14. Expect down markets and financial recessions and use them as a buying opportunity with stocks on sale.
15. Diversify your investments using mutual funds or ETFs to reduce the volatility of your investment portfolio.
16. Be more aggressive in your stock allocation when young, and initiate a more conservative asset mix (ie. add bonds) as you age, and your investment time horizon shortens.
17. Make provision for your retirement savings of 15% of income prior to investing for your child's education.
18. Invest in a 529 College Savings plan to assist your children to attend college without acquiring massive student loan debt.
19. Purchase a home you can afford without strangling your budget and becoming house poor. Your mortgage and related expenses should be no more than 25-30% of your take home pay.
20. Give generously to others in need, as the Lord blesses you!

The LORD bless you and keep you;
The LORD make His face shine upon you
And be gracious to you;
the LORD turn His face toward you
And give you peace.

NUMBERS 6:24-26

STUDY GUIDE ANSWER KEY

LESSON 1

birth
no
short
loved, whoever
name
spare, all
every
word
faithful
prosper, pray
earnestly, prosperous
obedience, prosperity
everything, prosperous
future
blessed
sought
more
enduring
chosen

LESSON 2

same
do not
remain
are
will
false
one
words
all
right
wisdom
wiser
depth
forgiving
God
compassionate
gracious
good
do
all
gracious
His
love
know
perish
unlimited
just, no
right
show
ways
LORD
all
unblemished
Every
provides
mindful
peace
peace
exalted
comes
living
eternal
dominion
discipline
ignores
despise
carefully
plan
self-controlled
worldly
all
hard
nothing
thought
transformed
pattern
pleased
guides
securely
heart
wisdom
marked
perseverance, not
steadfast
make
set out
settled, own
himself
account
gaze
fix
words
honest
look
honest
treasure
heart
offensive
required, trust
much
delights
keep
clear
respect
everything
generously
come
prosper
himself
Your
undivided

LESSON 3

always
care
toil
own, gift
distributes
skillful
use, serve
skill, work
favor, work
satisfaction
good, advance
everything
nothing
lot, toil
household
labor
blessed
rested, all
not
regular
unwilling
refuse
slack
awake
ways
finds
labored
diligent
poverty
wholeheartedly
reaps
great
well
anxious, grief
wear, harvest
sincerity, will, serving
everything, reverence
obligation
worth
content
agree
capital, completion

LESSON 4

everything
comes
belongs, given, forever
needed
return
heaven, heart
best
firstfruits
reluctantly, cheerful
gladly
willing, freely
moved
prompts
desire
No one
offering
proportion
acceptable
keeping
grace
tenth
tenth
tenth
tithe
all
everything
Test, blessing
overflowing
spare
open
given, over
offerings
accepts
no
meaningless

LESSON 5

save
gain
hinders
worthless
discipline
wanders
enslaved
conform, will
pleasant, peace
crucified
self-controlled
attention
careful, holes
you
always
knowledge
beneficial, not
desires
abundance
nothing
heart
satisfied
richest
gluttons
ways, flesh
attitude, like
divided
itself
worry, knows
let
lack
contentment, content
every, all
all
lack
loses

LESSON 6

everything, Wealth
belongs
comes
works
anyone
satisfy
enough
lack
bless
desires
not

knowledge
nothing
indulge
pretend
examines
wasting
will
given
trusted, handling
demanded
anything

wise
envy
slays
respite
mastered
imitated
ignorance
word
true, last
right, walk
security

no
pledge, pay
creditors
slave
all
pledge, not
sold
lead, paths
your

LESSON 7

surely
you will
EVERY
DESTINED
prepared

warn
secure, complacent
follow, anxious, sure
careful, SUDDENLY
refuge

sustain
DELIVERS
pray
discouraged, blameless
safety

reserve
reserved

LESSON 8

deposit
invest
AT ONCE
outrageous
oppose
cleverness
opposing
destitute
greedy
chase, poverty

myths, train
did not, reaped
wisdom, returns
wisdom
knowledge
trusting
speculative, no
prosperous
sure, certain
unseen

hope, patient
wealth
invest, determined
put in
cannot
sell
tranquility
top, bottom
little, little
endurance

hopes, wait
patient
understanding
everything
God
difficult
differently

LESSON 9

generation
good way
again, done
foretell
hope, God
NO ONE
discover, comprehend
yet to come

ruin
downfall
go out
surely
melted
one hour
gone
acquired

fool
rise
hope in
as well as
anything
firm
trust
on behalf

steadfast
doubt
stand still
will
more
restore

LESSON 10

succeed
many

sleep, ruin
little, little

proper, procedure
all

LESSON 11

themselves, wisdom
ways, paths
all your, submit, straight
view, know
plan, steps
two
share
divided
reason

rational, Reasonable,
essential
wisdom
diligent
wisdom, knowledge
understanding,
judgement
right

straightforward, plan,
spend, costs, risk
amount, time, return,
diversification
risk
five, fail
goals, guides, repeatable
principles, guide, know

investments, plan,
reactions, decisions
you, most, tolerance,
investor
according, reality, few
diligence
persevere
everything
prosperity

LESSON 12

mirror, biases, know
thyself, investor
opposite
best, risks, avoided,
neglect
control, sudden
invest, smartest
discipline, behave, you
odds, maximize,
behavior
partial, ready

impulsively, blind, trans-
forming
stock
sustained, predictive,
volatility
tendency, poor, good
Cycles, today's
predictable
no
better, higher, riskier,
better

losses, risk, safety
succeeded, skill
confident
highly, sober
rising, low, everyone,
instincts
conversation, worst
sheep
losses, twice
possibility
one, four

admitting, sell, alive
assume
successful, winners,
whole
overvalue
agree
right now
irresistible, powerful

LESSON 13

careful, major
shelter, refuge
ready, buying
settle
homes
five, closing, upfront
emergency, beyond
carefully, thousands
affordable, five
score, favorable, best
conventional
credit, interest, one, bills,
maxing
first, fewer
less, more
down, letter, back
purchase, escrow, loan
closing
2-3
really
bank, two, emergency
cash, waiting
thorough, update
verified, donor
ready
not, escrowed

carry
down
comparisons, contact,
lenders
half, negotiate, wiggle,
buy, lower
point, even, pay
huge, subtle, multiple,
total
interest-only, afford, reset
inflationary, payment,
peace
cash, free, principal
conditional, competitive,
letter, date
take, sum
gross, trouble, buyers,
financial, entirety
stretch, job, 10%
calculator, ballpark,
payment, refine
struggle, credit
top, important, expensive,
joy, outside
common, rooms, need,
risk

value, $3000
sag
renting, flexibility
acquire
provide
wherever
exactly, open
exact
walked, followed
before, appeal, best,
worst, retail, nicer
God, lacks
sought, built
property
long
alone, buyer, areas, offer,
hot
legally, best, listens, good
realistic, willing, 85%
can't, skills, cash, sell,
budget
terms, contingencies,
inspection, home, greater
advantage
inspected, code,
structure, walk, ask

survey
through, God
deep, well
stands
inspector, free
exit, withdraw, full, buyer
finances, income,
charging, not
required, disclosure, sign
understand
deed, silver, terms, safe,
fortunes
equity, servicer, save
reassessed, taxes
predict, time, bidding,
mistake, competitive
perspective, inflationary,
inflation, appreciation,
rent
scale, foregone, diluting
small
less, richer, lost, perform
stock, costs, lower

LESSON 14

righteousness
life
wife, next
enjoy
transformed, perfect
abundantly
task, testifying
always
goal

life, rich
extension, satisfying
tithing, 15%, insurance
money, while, will
investment, 25, lacking
Net Worth, measure
greater, ideal
probable, full, sustain

secret, stress, joyful,
lifetime, annuity
all
less, aggressively,
portfolio
length, asset, risk, most
uninformed, retirement
budgeting, ~85%
equity, one

retirement, online
income, withdrawals
Monte Carlo, probable
throughout, accurate
projected, singleness,
well
following
40%, ~8%

replaced, neutral, unless,
rate
optimal, half
long, expected
end
appointed
life
power
secure, anything
saved, 25%, workers
discern
investing, compound
prosperity

online
save, goal
decumulation, diligently,
spending, values,
memories
fixed, using, disciplined,
life
safe, retiree
fixed, 3.3, low,
overvalued
change, weakness, forgo,
declines

flexible, limits, decrease,
performance, enlarging
10%, reduce, value,
bequest
protect, outliving
investment, decline,
forced, especially
risk, expected, equity
higher, separate, need
minimizing, propor-
tional

needs, lifestyle, conser-
vatively, sequence, shares,
growth
lost, replace, never
nearer
personal, giving
assets, less, charitable
bunch, tax, wise
qualified
legacy, overextending,
deduction
wealth

LESSON 15

risk, unexpected
feared, peace
metrics, premium, many
deductible, wise, below,
higher
you, ransom, suddenly
damage
accident, group, bang
High, percentage, usage,
value
young, needs, tax, grows,
medical, averse
need, spending, tax
require, each, injury,
property
person, damage
partial, still, bills, file
collides, out, unexpected

easily, plus, outright
personal
home
on
largest, current
attached
never
known
flood
limits, 10%, actually
in, limit, 50-70%,
inventory
lawsuits, responsible,
umbrella
loss
away, hotel, all, beyond
rider
disasters, distinct

weather, value, credit
belongings, renters
disability, off,
permanently, 4, disabled
income, qualifying,
benefit, waiting
unable, return, doctor,
how, unexpected
60%, terms
rely
know, little, Lord's
time
clear, income, stability
period, less, costs, invest
age, chronic
secure
premium, financial
untimely, without

wealth
security, 15, costly
expensive
70%, worry
invest, premium
living, two, designed
average, savings
outlive
period, 3, 3%
deductible, qualified
life, death, not
60
yourself, old, lead
liability, personal
wrongs, full
assets, limits, relatively,
Net Worth
target, more

LESSON 16

tax, diligence
any, regard
chunk, big, retain,
fluctuated, entire, 8%
important, small, highly,
actively, must, dividends,
higher
submit, by God, pay,
time, owe
spiritually
government, taxes

in, out, pre-tax, Required,
after
large, choose
withdrawals, growth
Roth, spousal, current,
minds, hold
investing, loan
fifth, food
according
excessive, consequences,
handicap, distribute, full
three, net, superiority

index, held
bonds
more, taxable
asset
maximum
sheltered, many, income
catch-up
appropriate, free
itemize
7.5%, end
itemize, single
managing, distributions

giving
directly, distribution,
yearly
trust, possibly, longevity
10%, learn
start, deferred, above,
burden
proportional
strategy
now, cash
loser, losses, offset, erase,
wash

LESSON 17

choose
hour
knowing
estate, we
house
number
legal, passing, trust, title
neglect
nothing
distributed, detail,
contingent

death
decide, financial
probate, dispute,
passwords
overlooked, privacy, time,
property
decisions, medical,
unable
terminal, don't, care
retirement, passed, their
belong

precedence
jointly, instructions
online
belong, funeral
changed, tax
providing, affected,
costly, aspect
during
preparing
happen, top
secure

regular, wealth
continue
unexpected, twice, clarity
burden, meetings,
equipped, principles
record, each
simplify

LESSON 18

belong, bless
all, need
satisfy, satisfy, never
wrong, treasures
others, your
grace
freely
act

give
more, withholds
refreshes
blessed
life
hope, God, generous
complete
love

actions
advance
expressing
tire
desire, deed
devote, urgent
doing
family

weary
power
dead
together
completion
sight
forget
share

least
needy
blessed
freely, gifts
reward
kind
give, nothing
all, open-handed

hands
tightfisted
prayer
share, righteousness,
rear, answer
blameless
keep
righteousness

rich
poverty
give
serve
rich, able
poor
know
kindly

food
not
lifted
needy
generous, thanksgiving,
thanks, sharing

www.ingramcontent.com/pod-product-compliance
Lightning Source LLC
Chambersburg PA
CBHW081817200326
41597CB00023B/4286

* 9 7 9 8 8 9 8 1 8 0 2 0 1 *